57 Buttermilk Acres

Martingale
Create with Confidence

57 Buttermilk Acres

Mixing Vintage &
New for a Cozy,
Inviting Home

Stacy
West

57 Buttermilk Acres:
Mixing Vintage & New for a Cozy, Inviting Home
© 2022 by Stacy West

18939 120th Ave. NE, Ste. 101
Bothell, WA 98011-9511 USA
ShopMartingale.com

Printed in Hong Kong
27 26 25 24 23 22   8 7 6 5 4 3 2 1

Library of Congress Cataloging-in-Publication Data is
available upon request.

ISBN: 978-1-68356-200-9

MISSION STATEMENT

We empower makers who use fabric and yarn
to make life more enjoyable.

CREDITS

PUBLISHER AND
CHIEF VISIONARY OFFICER
Jennifer Erbe Keltner

CONTENT DIRECTOR
Karen Costello Soltys

PRODUCTION MANAGER
Regina Girard

COPY EDITOR
Taylor ffitch

COVER AND
BOOK DESIGNER
Angie Haupert Hoogensen

DESIGN MANAGER
Adrienne Smitke

PHOTOGRAPHER
Adam Albright

SPECIAL THANKS
*Photography for this book was taken at the
author's home in Minneapolis, Minnesota.*

If home is where your heart is, then why not make it a place that's warm, inviting, and filled with the people and things you love most?

contents

BIG IDEAS 11

SIGNATURE SPACES.............103

My goal is to help you discover how to turn your home into an inviting space filled with those things that speak to your heart.

SMALL PLACES

COLLECTIONS

introduction

I have many happy memories associated with home growing up. Those feelings are likely what drove me as an adult to make our family home memorable for all the days, not just the holidays. Over the years, I've enjoyed collecting a range of vintage items and I still enjoy a little retail therapy looking for new pieces to mix into our home decor. And, like you, I've turned to books, magazines, and websites for ideas.

But what was often missing for me was understanding *how* to put the items together in a pleasing way. For some, building a look is intuitive, but from other friends I hear "I don't know how you do it. I love how inviting this looks, but I could never figure out how to put it all together." My answer: Yes. You. Can.

I'm here to share with you a variety of ways to decorate everything from the permanent fixtures in your home to the smallest of nooks. You'll have oodles of ideas for not only *what* to do, but *how* to do it yourself. You absolutely can learn the basics of creating your own signature style.

If you love creating a cozy home for yourself and your family, and mixing new and old finds, you've come to the right place. Welcome to 57 Buttermilk Acres.

big ideas

What spaces in your home set the tone for the look and feel you love? Ideally, it's the places where you and your family spend the most time. Those places are also likely the most public spaces that guests see. In our home, those places are the family room, the kitchen, and the dining room. What follows is a framework for how I pull them together with new and old pieces that speak to my heart. I hope these pages speak to your heart, too.

11

Timeless
Treasures

≪ *Don't let a chip, ding, scratch, or less-than-perfect surface keep you from collecting pieces with unique textures and designs. On more than one occasion I've cracked a frame edge, spot-glued it together, and kept on decorating.*

Your home, like mine, may have symmetrical structural items like a mantel centered on one wall and two recessed windows over built-in cabinets. For some, symmetry speaks to the soul and the equal balance creates a sense of calm. But others, like me, struggle with symmetry. Here's why: as a collector, I often buy decor items in multiples, such as the vintage clock faces in this display, but I rarely buy two of the exact same item. I enjoy making balanced displays that aren't made from identical pieces on both sides.

Let me deconstruct the mantel arrangement on pages 12 and 13 to give you an idea of how I build this look in our home.

I generally begin with a theme or season in mind. For this look I wanted something seasonless that could stay in place for a time. My color inspiration began with the chunky wood pillars and columns. The details and lines in the pieces are eye-catching. From there I brought in an assortment of frames. Again, I love the detailed carvings and lines. Including both natural wood and chippy white frames helped me lighten the overall look a bit. The natural wood tones of the permanent mantel also help highlight the lighter framed elements. Though I could have left the empty frames open, I opted to showcase a collection of vintage clock faces by hanging each on hand-dyed ribbon in the negative space of the frame openings. I love the juxtaposition of the circles with the squares.

Next up, I added in a variety of live and faux plants to add both height and a pop of Mother Nature's best goes-with-everything color—green.

I like to play with odd numbers in my decorating, but that doesn't mean you have to avoid even numbers. For example, there are four frames but just three clock faces (seven total).

To balance the side displays, I incorporated old corbels and other architectural salvage in chippy whites on both sides of the mantel. The cubby with drawers on the left is sometimes used in our home as a table (see page 179), but here I raised it to be a dramatic anchor on the left—a foil to the antique birdcage, urn, and sap bucket of natural twigs on the right.

When you have a multi-drawer cabinet, pull out drawers to create a shelf as I did, resting the ceramic swan atop a book. Other drawers are opened slightly to hold a wood croquet ball (the same color as the chunky pillars) and another clock face (repeating an item from the mantel's center). The little white chest of drawers helps break up the dark expanse of the larger anchor cupboard.

On the right side, I repeated the rounded cloche shape with the vintage birdcage, and the seltzer

» *Layer, layer, layer! I needed to lighten up and level the bottom of the birdcage before setting the urn inside, so I added a round framed mirror that forms the perfect base to complete the look. It introduces contrast without attracting too much attention.*

> *I gradually gathered these pieces from antique stores, estate sales, and Etsy shops. I rotate them in and out of my decor depending on the season and the mood I'm after.*

bottle's soft oval shape. There's another clock face to add a cohesive element.

To soften the overall look, a small throw is nested in the basket at the bottom corner of the fireplace. One of my favorite elements is the ivy trailing from an old plant stand. To me it feels like I'm bringing the past back into our home. What was this piece? Maybe it held a spray at a wedding, or perhaps a funeral? I don't know, but I love it. The sweeping vines add organic movement and soften the hard lines of the other pieces.

An open drawer is the perfect spot to tuck visual delights into a display. Use books or other small flat objects to make a base atop open drawers to create a little shelf.

Date
Night

❝

Show someone how special they are to you by decorating a space to celebrate with them. It's a labor of love in the place you love most.

❞

57 BUTTERMILK ACRES

Your home should be the place where you're happiest; the spot where memories are made and joys are celebrated. I look back fondly at gathering three generations of family around the table, and of course, holiday festivities. I strive to make all the rooms in our home joyful spaces, and you don't need a special occasion to make a memory. I couldn't think of a better way to celebrate with my husband than setting up a little date night scenario where we could enjoy each other's company in the coziest of places— our home.

My vision was a romantic Paris cafe setting. Keeping with that theme, the mantel is a mix of vintage finds (can you imagine them perhaps gathered from a Parisian flea market?) and lush plants that mimic an alfresco dining experience. I like to think of the bird print in the center of the mantel as a pair of love birds. Vintage rattan-covered wine bottles allude to a restaurant setting and the pampas grass filling them adds a feathery lightness to the overall look. Except for two dark architectural elements on the mantel, I chose a mix of chippy white corbels, candlesticks, and wood pieces to fill the remaining space with calming texture that doesn't call too much attention to itself.

Switching things up by not setting up our date night at the kitchen or dining-room table, I instead centered a decorative iron table in front of the

FINISHING TOUCHES

Concealing the bases of plants can get spendy and more than a little messy if you're keen to keep the look natural. I've tried green moss and Spanish moss, but I'm often dissatisfied with the effect and coverage. But a little crafty ingenuity was all it took for this look, reusing wrapping from an online purchase. The honeycomb packing paper became the perfect reuse-and-recycle filler needed to cover the plant pot. The natural hue was on point and the texture added interest!

⌃ Visual weight is determined by the density and opacity of your decor items, or by the use of darker, rich colors. To lighten the overall look, consider monochromatic neutral objects in white or cream.

fireplace. A pair of cozy, soft chairs flanks either side. A vintage scale helps elevate the look with a natural basket and plant on one side of the table and an appetizer plate of fruits and veggies on the opposite side. A charcuterie board of meats and cheeses was in the refrigerator, ready to pair with the bread basket options. A couple of vintage linens for napkins and a table runner soften and warm up the look. If I hadn't set this up in the summertime, I might have added a few tapers here and there for a candlelight glow. All in all, we enjoyed the space, the company of one another, and not having to leave home. Isn't that why we all love to create inviting spaces? 🍂

Whether it's a special occasion or an everyday celebration, sink into the simple joys of your home by creating spaces to spend time together with your most important people.

DATE NIGHT

Spring
Awakening

Minnesota springtime means I'm beyond ready to bring the outside in. This arrangement may have begun before the bulbs were coming up outside, but I couldn't wait any longer!

The foundation pieces I started with were the insurance sign (those colors!) and the two pieces of children's metal lawn furniture. Having one chaise and one chair meant having a couple of "same but different" pieces for opposite sides of the display—my favorite! Spring bulbs and flowering plants did most of the heavy lifting when it came to adding color and life to the overall decor, but chippy white urns, a lawn ornament (the sunbonnet gal on the left has a base added for indoor use), cloches, and birdhouses add to the seasonal mix.

It's rare for me not to include a little cupboard or two for height and variety, as I did on the right side of the mantel. Opening the drawers to tuck in some natural elements adds an extra layer of interest. Finally, the clay pots scattered throughout tie in well with the color of my floors and are, for me, a harbinger of many trips to the nursery ahead.

The pillars at the base of the fireplace provide a visual anchor, but their happy spring green

《 *Vintage trophies or loving cups can be high-ticket finds these days. For a thriftier solution, try searching for a silver plated champagne bucket instead.*

> 66
>
> *Ordinary objects become artful objects when displayed under a cloche. Decorate with cloches year-round, and don't limit yourself to placing them over plants.*
>
> 99

⌃ *The streamlined silhouettes of the multi-drawer pieces provide the ideal backdrop for a variety of organic items with just enough contrast and texture for a visual pop in small spaces.*

color helps to keep them visually light. The third birdhouse perched atop one of the pillars brings a cohesive element to the entire display and makes for an odd number of pieces, which I love.

Overall, it's a lighter, brighter look than I sometimes live with, but at this time of year, I'm ready for it! 🌼

Friends have come to expect the unexpected when they get an up-close look at how I use my finds in displays. Hats off to you if you like to have the same kind of fun!

A vintage Easter bonnet (above right) became the perfect riser for a small potted plant beneath a cloche (bottom). It was the tiny fabric blossoms on the hat that caught my eye first. Incorporating it in a spring display felt natural. Placing the hat under glass felt a bit like placing a jewel in a box, making it even more special. Giving the pot a little boost to better fill out the cloche was a plus, too. With the hat's combs tucked underneath, no one can guess the bonnet's former life until I point it out to them.

Harvest
Season

It's hard for me to turn away from any porch post segments, but this trio might just be my all-time favorite. I flew home with them in a suitcase. They were too special to pass up!

Fall is my favorite of the four seasons. Farm stands filled with the season's bounty, crisp air, and changing leaves are fuel to the fire when it comes to my desire to cozy up our home. The twisted porch-post segments turned pumpkin perches are the spark that ignited this look. Incorporating the organic textures of pumpkins, gourds, dried cornstalk leaves, bittersweet, and kale is a natural choice. Pairing metal sap buckets with salt-glazed pottery crocks and jugs gives an outdoorsy edge to the entire display.

Don't be afraid to combine new finds and old treasures. Vintage purists might tell you there are rules to collecting and displaying your finds, but I'm all about mixing new and vintage together to tell *your* story. I purchased the custom-painted sign above the mantel new. There are some fabulous signmakers I've met through social media who make new signs that look old, complete with chippy paint and rusty discolorations. The sign became the center focal point between two sides of the mantel that mirror one another.

Though the sizes of the crocks and buckets aren't exact pairs, they still mix well. A few curly twigs and a single peacock feather on each side add wispy height. Sprays of pheasant feathers add a richer, moodier element than fall flowers would. Pine cones are more commonly used in winter settings, but they can bring a fun feel to fall too. To carry the look down to the hearth, an additional crock is filled with dried corn stalk leaves. On the

⌃ *Though my crocks were different sizes, I did add up the stamped gallon numbers on each side to equal eight (4+4 and 5+3). That's one way to achieve balance!*

» *Garden centers can be every bit as exciting as junk bonanzas and flea markets when it comes to finding plants, dried flowers, and natural elements.*

> *When decorating a space, try to think of it as if the room is telling a story.*
> *It might be about the people who live here or about an upcoming event.*

opposite side, a vintage wire basket holds a collection of wood mashers. Bringing the kitchen into the setting? Yep, because I like mixing in the wood tones. I'm not worried about the literal uses of my collections. If they have the right look and feel, there's a way to mingle them together.

The last major element of this look is a pair of rusty white candelabras that have the perfect patina, adding a rustic elegance to the scene. The slightest pop of fall color is added with mustard-gold tapers. A cozy autumnal throw and a pair of plaid pillows complete an inviting look that has me ready to curl up with a good book and a cup of hot cocoa. How about you?

PICK YOUR OWN   OPEN SAT & SUN
WEST FAMILY FARMS
PUMPKINS
HAYRIDES CORN MAZE CIDER & MORE

Winter
Wonderland

I have oodles of Christmas decor in seasonal reds and greens, but sometimes I want a wintry look that lasts beyond the holidays. Reverting to a neutral palette means I can keep the look well past the start of a new year. Using cream and gold trees gives them a frosty, wintry look, and evergreens are everlasting in the Northern states where I live.

When decorating a mantel, give consideration to the height of your tallest elements for a good starting point. Here, I began with the frames at the center and knew I wanted the overall look to flow from top right to bottom left, mixing up the arrangement from my other looks.

From there, I pulled in the biggest pieces and began building. Some tips to consider when decorating your own mantel:

» **Texture:** Consider bringing in some softness (like the wool felt deer on page 39).

» **Contrast:** This look uses a mix of old and new champagne buckets and trophies/loving cups for tree stands.

» **Form over function:** Don't be afraid to leave candlesticks unfilled. They can be decorative elements on their own to bring shape and color. You don't have to fill them.

» **Numbers:** The mantel has three gold trees and five cream trees, both odd numbers. Then there's the greenery: one garland + two larger trees = three green items.

» **Accent colors:** Repeated secondary colors can play a supporting role. The black frame of the fireplace led me to include a couple of black accent pieces in the display. ✤

⌃ *Keeping to a neutral, timeless palette of colors and textures leaves plenty of room for the season to shine through with familiar tree shapes, the warmth of candlelight, and the glimmer of mixed metals.*

⩾ Stacks of vintage suitcases add texture and height. If you're lucky enough to find a suitcase with an interesting interior, prop it open in your display. Alternatively, suitcases can do double duty storing out-of-season items not currently in use.

> Choose materials, textures, and colors that are warm and inviting to your eye. No green thumb? No worries. You might be surprised at just how many fabulous faux greenery options you can find.

Welcome Home

» *What constitutes a serving tray? Anything flat and level, in my book! Turn a clipboard you love into a one-of-a-kind beverage station.*

What's the first space guests see in your home when they walk through the front door? In our home, the dining room is situated just off the main entryway, which means it sets the tone for how the house feels to guests. To that end, I love to create a welcoming first impression that alludes to what they'll see as they step farther inside.

I purposefully chose a mix of chairs and bench seating, knowing we love to entertain. Not only does the bench graciously make room for more at the table, but it also can provide a decorating opportunity when no one's seated there. By choosing two different styles of chairs, if we need to bring in a few more from around the house at the holidays, the additions won't stand out as being the only mismatched seats at the table. Again, that's a small touch, but one that makes for a more inviting table.

This is not our everyday table, but we do host guests often, so creating a setup for a buffet gives me the jump when an impromptu gathering arises. I chose to center the display with the metal circle on the wall as a backdrop. It's a staple in my dining room. To me, it reads like the perimeter of a clock face without any of the inner markings or timepiece. I loosely laid out a round vintage tablecloth and let it spill off the front edge of the tabletop, breaking the visual line that runs the length of the table. From there, a large, rectangular wire basket gives shape to the

A splash of gold adds a little dazzle to any look. A treasured cookbook rests on the easel now, but imagine a menu card there when the party starts.

centerpiece, but doesn't add much visual weight. It delineates a space that allows for the layered look I love. The cloche holding the neutral thread balls could easily be replaced by a cake or charcuterie board atop the cake stand when a party commences.

Live plants and their fabulous faux counterparts are enjoying a resurgence in popularity, which means finding the ideal shape and size to complement (but not overwhelm) your table is easier than ever.

I propped my plant on the dining table in a champagne bucket to give it more height. A stack of plates, a few drinking glasses, and a few of my favorite vintage finds complete the ensemble.

All in all, it's a compact, layered vignette that I hope invites closer inspection by visitors who enjoy the delights of making their house a home as much as I do. Pull up a chair or make yourself comfortable on the bench. Welcome! 🌿

« The sideboard setup doesn't repeat the same elements as the tabletop. Instead it's the neutral palette of the objects that holds the look together. An old magazine rack holds vintage crocks and baskets. And I'm all in for typography, signs, and ephemera.

⌃ Details matter. Dress up a dress form with her own fun baubles for an accessory success!

Spring
Forward

Casual yet sophisticated looks that elevate the everyday spaces in your home convey an easygoing vibe so your guests can relax and enjoy. The inspiration for this look began with a mix of old and new that I wanted to use at each place setting—butterfly chocolate molds and papier-mache carrots with raffia tops.

First off, remember that not all table setups need to be symmetrical. Do you ever host dinner for a smaller group but don't want to spread out across a big table? Here the table is set for five,

When nesting pieces, add unexpected twists like the flocked bunnies tucked into antique funeral baskets filled with twig wreaths, spring florals, and greenery.

⌃ *Every great display starts with a story I tell myself. An artist's loft, where spring bursts forth on canvas and a pitcher of brushes invites continued creativity. Cement bunnies add a touch of whimsy. The painting held by the antique easel is new, but the tones and colors perfectly complement the overall look.*

and the extra space at one end is used to create a spring look that lasts. Positioning the bench on the opening side of the dining room allows it to become another inviting surface to decorate. A long, low basket brimming with treasures is easily picked up and set aside at a moment's notice without the hassle of having to dismantle a vignette piece by piece when your guests arrive.

The beautiful, delicate handwork along the edges of vintage linens catches my eye every time. Collecting and using linens in nestled settings like this one is great because their size doesn't matter.

They don't have to fit your table; you just have to love their look. If there's a little hole or stain, no worries. Fold and drape a favorite piece from a basket, or softly unfurl it to create gentle fabric curves beneath your display.

If holiday decor suits your style, this look is certainly adaptable to a full-on Easter celebration with the addition of some pastel eggs or chocolate bunnies. But if you like to let your decor linger for weeks rather than days, use fewer holiday-themed pieces and allow for a segue into spring that can be enjoyed for a couple of months. 🌼

« *A European cutting board with intricate carvings becomes an artist's palette for holding a flower frog turned brush stand and tiny pitcher one might expect to be filled with water for dipping a brush.*

Summer
Fun

*Are you a dish collector like I am?
Prop open a small suitcase and stack
some summery place settings where
you can see and enjoy them!*

Take me out to the ball game, take me out with the crowd. It's all fun and games when summertime comes. The days are long and we enjoy grilling and chilling with friends, so this look brings the outdoors in with some casual fun. As a collector of vintage tins, two things catch my eye— the typography and the color. The tin I started with here was the red check one, which brought to mind a picnic tablecloth. From there, I was on a mission to snap up any tins I could find that were mostly red. The Campfire Marshmallow tin took me back to my childhood days of s'mores, so I added in a few wooden skewers and a plate of marshmallows for roasting to the table.

What's your sport, baseball or softball? Both are showcased here. Vintage balls, well-scuffed of

Vintage soda pop bottles take me back to my younger days too. The names and the clever use of fonts and logos just spell summer fun! But any time you have a clear glass bottle in a big display, you risk losing the charm of the typography unless you add a filler to help make the text pop. What's my solution to add the perfect finishing touch? Add some white beans to fill the bottles partway and a few candy-striped paper straws to make it look as if the kids are halfway through sipping their sodas. That does the trick!

course, are a flea market find and I love the dots of rounded happiness, spread out across the tabletop, looking like they just rolled in off the diamond. But you could just as easily plan a golf-lover's look with a couple of vintage woods, tees, and a bucket of golf balls. Or maybe you'd prefer to serve up some tennis with a couple of old wooden racquets and a few tennis balls instead. Developing a theme is really about creating a story in your mind's eye about a topic you or your guests can get enthused about. The thrill of the hunt for old-time treasures is part of the fun!

I'm always looking for ways to add height and a touch of drama to any display, so some small vintage suitcases and a scale provide just the right boost here. Serve up a bowl of Cracker Jack and peanuts-in-the-shell and see if a fun summer's eve isn't on deck for you and your friends!

If you don't have a formal dining room and your everyday table isn't a possibility to hold a bigger display like this for an extended time, think about other places in your home where you can pull off a look like this. Consider these options:

» Atop a table in your entryway
» On a sofa table behind a couch
» Above a bookshelf in your office
» On a small chest at the end of a hallway
» Inside a covered porch or portico 🎴

《 Time out! The adjacent sideboard setting pairs two of my related collections—clock faces and alarm clocks.

Where to begin? It's clear by now that I'm a collector. If one is good, three are better, and ten are great! But we all must start somewhere, and what do you do if you only have a single clock face in your collection? I think that placing any object under glass elevates its status immediately. So, I've tucked my clock face in a lidded jar nestled in a bed of dominoes. Why dominoes? Humor me. You count the dots on dominoes. A clock face is counting time. Get it? It makes me smile. And the addition of the trivet beneath the jar elevates the look, literally and figuratively. Trust me, you can turn solo treasures into stars.

Autumn Glow

Harvest season brings all the fall feels into our homes. Pumpkin spice might not be my thing, but a trip to the pumpkin patch definitely is! And the plethora of heirloom-variety pumpkins in so many soft fall colors takes my breath away. A wagonload of pumpkins can go a long way to creating a lasting autumnal look.

My fall dining table includes a pair of plump pillows and a cozy throw to warm up the space. While pumpkins and eucalyptus branches are the main attraction along the center of the table, a mix of Pottery Barn dishes in leaf, acorn, and pumpkin shapes proves you can mix new and old to create the look you love.

57 BUTTERMILK ACRES

« *Whether you set your table as a buffet or sit around it for dinner, varying the heights of serving pieces and layering them adds to the overall richness of your look, creating a more interesting feast for the eyes.*

66

When I set a table, I love to include a distinctive item at each place setting. It's a personal touch that shows my guests that no detail has been overlooked in creating a gathering and a meal they'll enjoy.

99

The rusty orange cubby atop the sideboard is the statement piece the entire dining room is centered around. For a change, I placed uniform items in each opening instead of my more common mix-and-match approach. It helps that all the little white pumpkins have variety in scale and in their stems. The perfectly imperfect look adds just a dash of whimsy.

To soften the grid of the cubbies and the sideboard drawers below, I nested a few simple items at the base of the cubbies, draping a fringed runner off the edge. To draw the eye toward the top of the cubbies, I let the organic shapes of the cornhusks and bittersweet sweep left and right. The vintage carnival game wheel is ideally suited to the season with its autumnal coloring for a look that is perfect from late September through early November. ⬧

⌃ *When choosing items from my collections to include in a display, I'm not looking for colors that match, but rather a range of colors that complement one another and the season.*

« *Mini orange pumpkins tucked into a vintage toy truck and a bundle of bright orange bittersweet add just the right pop of orange to counter the all-white pumpkin cubby lineup.*

Snow Days

⌃ *A wooden chicken feeder at the center of the table has built in risers, allowing decor elements to nestle up to and under the edge for a lush look.*

> 66
>
> *White reflects the sunlight, which many of us miss during short winter days, so mixing lighter elements on your tabletop adds an airy feel.*
>
> 99

Mixing modern and vintage is a happy marriage of styles that can't go wrong. My dining room wall already sets the tone with lots of character, so using a simpler setting for the table prevents the display from being overwhelming. But simpler doesn't have to mean sparse.

The look begins with a striped linen table runner framing the center of the table where the long and lanky chicken feeder becomes the center stage base. To play off the snowy season in Minnesota where I live, I add pops of white throughout with wax candle trees and modern white dishes. Three chunky candlesticks in natural wood tones add visual interest, but I purposefully set only two candles into the holders, leaving the center candlestick open. This lets the table be the focus, rather than directing your eye toward a tall center point.

Pine tree plates and glass baubles greet guests with a holiday nod, as do handmade silverware stockings. After the holidays, I remove the stockings.

The sideboard, a new piece that looks old, nestles in a space meant for a china cupboard. Its lower height affords the opportunity for dramatic, asymmetrical decor on top.

Mother nature's wintry showstoppers, green pines, appear here in multiple forms from boughs to tree shapes. The natural color of the vintage feather tree in the corner of the room inspired the addition of the deer to the woodland theme, as well as the natural wicker place mats. It's important to remember when you're mixing in elements on your table that color can play an equally important role as texture. Some might feel that wicker is for summer, but it fit in perfectly with this wintry look because the color matches the fawns and deer so well.

Pine tree pillows made from feedsacks and an old army blanket add a cozy touch to chairs at each end of the table. A woven throw gives guests a welcoming wrap to drape across a lap to take the chill off.

The holiday baubles on the garland, in the bowl, and on the sideboard tree are easily removed so the wintry look will last well into the new year, and the golden glimmer of the brass deer can be enhanced by adding a few votive candles to flicker on a frosty night.

STARTING POINT

Write it down: you can't go wrong when you collect vintage books to use as decor. They can be used in every room of the house and in multiple ways. If you're just getting started, consider these options:

» Though I can't bring myself to remove the bindings from old books, other people do and I'm thankful. The neutral patina and look of aged book pages sewn together in sections marries

well with vintage goods. You'll often find these when you're out junking at fairs or festivals.

» Look for titles, typography, and/or graphics you appreciate on the covers.

» Search for a range of covers in a color you decorate with frequently. Build a collection in that color palette, then move on to another hue.

Sweet and Simple

Lidded glass jars evoke a terrarium feel, so I played up that vibe by placing a single faux fern leaf inside as nature's perfect objet d'art.

Kitchens can be a challenge when it comes to integrating decor while maintaining functionality. In today's open-concept homes, kitchens are often seen from surrounding spaces and the separation between those spaces can be difficult to define. It's no different in our house, where a large island is all that separates the kitchen from the family room. I love that our family can be gathered in the same area while dinner is being made, but it means the family room and kitchen decor can't be wildly different in tone or it would be visually jarring.

To keep the look similar from one space to another during spring, I opt for a nature-inspired color scheme, rather than typical springtime pastels. I set the stage with some core pieces that are almost always on our open shelves—mortars and pestles, ironstone pitchers, and vintage glass apothecary jars.

For a pulled-together appearance, I like to treat the everyday appliances as supporting stars in the scene. To that end, I tucked the toaster into a champagne crate and perched our coffee maker atop an antique breadboard. Neither move inhibited their use, but it helped prevent the setup from looking as though all decor stopped below the shelving. You may notice many of the smaller pieces vary from white to cream. I don't worry one bit about mixing the two tones. It's a perfect pairing.

“

The paper on the clipboard is from February 17, 1930, a girl's
school report on bluebirds. The penmanship is exquisite.
Imagine what she'd think to know that it's here, nearly 100 years later.

”

SWEET AND SIMPLE

> **"** Don't underestimate the visual power of clear glass in decorating. Glass containers or objects add shape and soft edges without weighing down the overall look. **"**

Birds and nests are harbingers of spring, so their inclusion along with a few spring green ferns seems like a natural fit.

Adding a nod to the head hare of the season, I incorporate bunny-shaped covered glass dishes hopping this way and that on plate stacks and shelves. Topping off the look, vintage chocolate bunny figurines are an easy whimsical addition for a couple of weeks around Easter.

With this sweet and simple look, we can celebrate spring and still navigate the kitchen in functional ways every day. Adding a footed breadboard with a small neutral vignette on the island near the sink helps carry the spring theme forward as it transitions to our family room.

FINISHING TOUCHES

Details make the difference, especially when it comes to fillers for clear glass pieces. Filling jars with different tones and textures unearths layers of beauty throughout to liven up the look. Some of my fillers include vintage crepe paper garland, assorted beans, speckled faux eggs, polished rocks, and skittle pins. Return to the full photo on pages 72 and 73 to see how seamlessly the hidden treasures integrate.

Everyday
Ease

⌃ When you have an artful home, don't forget to spend some of your creativity on food presentation as well. Layer cutting boards and wrap bread with paper and twine. Remember, we eat with our eyes too!

Open shelving makes my heart go pitter-patter. If you're considering removing your upper cabinets and installing open shelves instead, I say go for it! Shelves offer a fantastic canvas upon which you can make your decorating mark in an often hard-to-embellish room, the kitchen.

Not everyone has the space to use open shelves for decor only. In fact, I'd guess the overwhelming majority of people need to have their everyday dishes at hand on open shelves. But there's no reason you can't mix artistic elements in with the items you use most often. It's functional and fun!

Every look begins with a seed of an idea, and for this one the stripes on the yellowware bowls were my starting point. The bowls set the stage for a tone-on-tone palette that lends an always-in-season approach to decorating with what you love. I made sure to incorporate everyday dishes into the most convenient spots before building in extras around them. Our family is tall, so the middle shelves provide the best option for plates, bowls, and drinking glasses. Tall glasses are turned upside down on the right to contrast with the similar-shape-but-shorter upright glasses in the wire caddy on the left-side shelves. To avoid too-tall stacks, a few extra bowls and plates were shifted to the lower-left shelf.

A collection of yellowware bowls and other treasured pottery pieces we use for baking and serving take places of honor throughout, shining

« If your objects don't have enough variation in scale, alter heights with items that fit your color palette. I chose a couple of books with covers removed and opted to turn and stack, rather than nest, a pair of bowls. Brown on brown can also lead to dark, heavy spots visually, so adding light plates or risers beneath brown bowls helps separate elements.

> " My family doesn't love that I decorate behind the cooktop. When it's filled with pots for cooking, we move the decor aside. But for me, it's a space that yearns to be adorned. So, I do! "

with their simple sophistication. House plants are enjoying a resurgence in popularity, and whether or not you have a green thumb for keeping them alive, an exceptional assortment of fabulous faux plants are now widely available and make managing your greenery a breeze. To repeat the color and texture of the wood shelving, a couple potato mashers and pestles add some curviness in small doses.

As always, it's important to connect the spaces by carrying the look to the counter below. Layering a scale atop an antique bread board makes the perfect perch for a small ironstone pitcher. 🌿

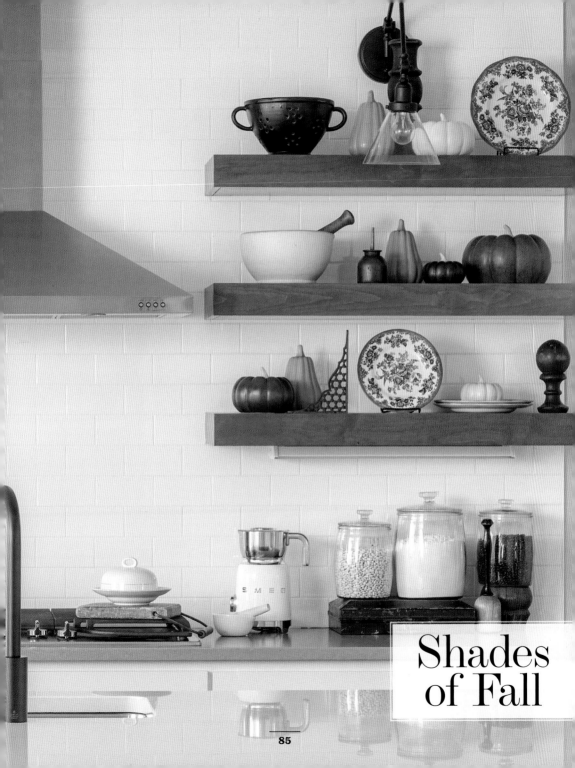

Shades
of Fall

I've no idea what the handled tray was actually meant for, but it adds just the right feeling to this setting.

A blend of beauty and functionality comes together in a look that was launched with a set of Royal Stafford black-and-cream plates. Mix in ceramic pumpkins in shadowy shades with a few black pottery pieces, a vintage iron shelf bracket, and my signature mortar and pestles and you've got a high-style, yet subdued setting.

Shaking up the appearance of your kitchen doesn't have to mean repainting the cupboards or replacing all your dishes. Maybe it's as simple as strategically placing a few select pieces, like these five stunning plates, upright on plateholders to draw attention. To be sure, I could just as easily have taken this look in a more elegant direction with silver service or crystal pieces, but I enjoyed the challenge of pairing these pretty pieces with matte pumpkins from Target and a local garden and gift center. The result is definitely a mix of modern and traditional that is on trend in today's home decor.

A few metal leaves flutter down as if falling from the sky. A couple of vintage oil cans and a finial or two complete the simple setup. The mug rack keeps coffee cups right at hand. And pantry staples that match the palette get a starring spot to the right of the stove.

Whooooo's that looking on from the island, overseeing the breakfast noshes? My guess is this vintage papier-mache fellow once had important work to do scaring off garden pests, but in my house, he's merely in charge of eyeballing the sweet treats. He looks positively parliamentary next to

⌃ *I love the juxtaposition of rustic, artisanal pieces paired with sophisticated china plates.*

the painted black pillar and he makes me chuckle every time I walk into the room. My advice? Don't take home decor too seriously. It's meant to be fun. And the next time you're out antiquing or junking and you see something that makes you smile, bring it home with you. Don't worry about what your plan for it is or where it will go. If you love it, you'll make it happen. I can assure you that I didn't have a vision for this owl when I first brought him home. Then, like a harvest moon in October, an idea arose and now he's perched right here!

If you want to pursue these ideas but aren't sure how to make it happen because you may not have open shelving or a kitchen island, don't despair. Rest assured, I've also lived for many years with traditional cupboards and that didn't slow my style. I worked with what I had. If you don't have open shelving in your kitchen but love the look, consider these alternatives:

» Is there a place where you can remove one cabinet from your kitchen to install open shelving instead? There are plenty of artisan shelf makers who also make invisible mounting brackets that pair easily with their shelves to complete the look.

» Can you clear a counter area beneath a bank of cabinets to set up a smaller seasonal vignette? Trays and shallow baskets are a great way to contain your treasures and keep your display looking just right.

» Do you have open space between the top of your cabinets and the ceiling? Often the tops of cabinets are recessed a few inches, but adding a few hidden risers (I've used old books and magazines) to boost items will help.

> "Don't overthink it. If you get stuck when you're decorating a space, walk away and come back to it later. Close your eyes and envision what could be. A fresh eye will help you achieve the look you want."

« I bought this metal box for its low height and for the patina on the outside of it, imagining I'd use it as a riser. I didn't even open it until I got home. Imagine my surprise to find it was an artist's oil painting kit with a palette, paints, and sketches still inside.

Natural
Effect

⌃ *Do be mindful of pieces that aren't labeled food safe. My workaround is to use parchment wrappers beneath the goodies.*

Seemingly ageless and as classic as it comes, ironstone has caught the eye of many collectors over the years and it's been enjoying a "moment" for what seems like a decade. Pottery, china, earthenware—ironstone comes in plenty of shapes and sizes. Many collectors stick to a single item, like pitchers, to focus their purchases. Not me. I'm all-in for all of it! Plates, check! Bowls and tureens, check! Serving platters, check!

I like the all-white pieces that have maintained their integrity of color through the years. I also swoon over the crazed and discolored pieces that almost look like they might have been factory mistakes. Rather than passing them by, I snap them up in appreciation of their lifetime of service. Whichever you prefer, when it comes to investing in a home-decor staple that you'll be able to enjoy for many years to come, you won't go wrong with ironstone. And even though I'm sharing a collection on display in my kitchen, ironstone can be at home in any room in your house. You can use pieces as vessels for bouquets or plants, as catchalls for keys near the door, or as simple stacks of objects to add shape and form to a shelf display.

Because I enjoy the patina of ironstone so much, I wanted these pieces to be the stars of the show in this kitchen arrangement. I began by balancing my largest pieces, placing at least one on each shelf in ways that keep the eye moving. For example, to the left of the stove, the tallest pot is on the top far left and I've turned a platter upright

ESTABLISHED 1874.

FRANK COOPER'S
"OXFORD"
HOME MADE
SEVILLE MARMALADE
WARRANTED PURE
PREPARED ONLY BY
Frank Cooper
OXFORD.

REGISTERED TRADE MARK.

66

The coolest part about crazing on pottery is that each piece becomes
unique in its patina and pattern over time. I embrace the discoloration
and individuality of these pieces because it speaks to their history.

99

NATURAL EFFECT

to act in tandem with a pitcher as a backdrop. Two similar-sized mortars and pestles are on opposite ends of the middle shelf, and a large bowl is centered on the lowest shelf. To the right of the stove, the pattern is slightly different with the largest elements creating a diagonal line from top left to bottom right across the three shelves.

Next, I layered in some smaller ironstone pieces, making sure to keep the variations in coloring dispersed across the entire look. If you struggle to see the subtle differences in tone when you're building your own displays, try using your cell phone camera to help. Take a picture, then convert it to black and white on your phone. Doing so makes it easier to determine if your lightest pieces and darkest pieces have enough contrast between them. Adjust accordingly.

Adding in plants usually means a mix of faux and real for me, and that was the next step. Most are in their original pots, but paired with an ironstone piece that hides everything except the greenery from view. This was intentional so that no dark pot rims compete with the soft tones of the ironstone.

The final touches are the most unexpected. Pieces of natural coral add texture and organic shape. A lacy black coral sea fan introduces a hint of black and a delicate element. Keeping the countertop clean and simple without extra embellishment puts all the focus right where I want it, on that gorgeous ironstone! 🪴

If you prefer a more minimalist look, remove the coral and the greenery and let the pottery pieces speak for themselves.

FRANK COOPER'S
OXFORD
SEVILLE MARMALADE

Forest
Frolic

Creating a wintry look that lasts from November through mid-February was the challenge I set for myself here. The hustle and bustle of the holidays is real, and as excited as I am to pull out all the stops to decorate the tree, when it's time to put the holiday decorations away, my enthusiasm sometimes wanes. So my goal was to set a winter scene, rather than to focus on Christmas-themed decor.

As mentioned in the "Sweet and Simple" kitchen on pages 72 and 73, you'll notice mortars and pestles are always on my kitchen shelves, along with some favorite ironstone pitchers. (In case you're wondering, our plates, bowls, and glasses are in lower cabinet sliding drawers.) I shared that my kitchen is an open-concept area adjacent to my family room, so you may want to take a second look at the "Winter Wonderland" pages 36 and 37 to see what's on the mantel wall opposite this kitchen shelving for the season.

This look is rooted in a neutral palette layered with wood tones, brass, stoneware, and pops of greenery. Putting it all together is a bit like putting together a puzzle. The tree shapes fit right

» *Elevate the ordinary by serving up your toast(er) on a silver platter. This little over-the-top touch makes my family smile every morning.*

⌃ *Vintage loving cups or trophies have become more spendy and difficult to find as collectors' interest increases. I'm partial to the smaller pieces perfect for holding frosty white trees that mimic Minnesota's wintry pines.*

FOREST FROLIC

"
A vintage candy box started
my concept for this wintry look.
Its earthy, reddish-brown tones, greens,
and creams guided my choices for
the overall color palette.
"

in for the holidays, but when I turn to January, I only need to pluck a tiny ornament or two from the tree on the counter and carry on.

Using multiples in a display is a designer trick sometimes called the "rule of three." The repetition of three elements in a setting is said to be most pleasing. I often use more than three of something, but try to keep an odd number of items—or in this case, odd numbers on each side of the center. There are 14 deer pieces in total, but seven per side. Having a balanced look doesn't have to mean equal numbers of pieces per side. Note that the two sides don't have even the same kinds of pieces to create a balance. There are no mortars and pestles on the left, while there are more books on the left than on the right. But, the two sides have balance in terms of their visual weight.

When you're mixing elements, if you find colors too similar, look for objects to separate like items. For example, the copper pot on the lower right is too similar in color to the shelf it rests on, so I placed it on a book with a dark cover to break apart the tones. Raising the copper pot really lets it shine, and the lift helps to better fill in the space between shelves.

Clear jars filled with inexpensive dried beans add texture and color without attracting too much attention, and pine cones add a great finishing touch. I love the variety of sizes and shapes to choose from, making them a great filler. 🍀

If you're on the fence about starting a collection because you're unsure what to do with a solo piece, don't fret. Sometimes a single piece is all you can find, all you want, or all you have space to keep. It doesn't mean you can't be a collector. It means you should love the one thing you're buying. A scale is versatile in so many settings because it can serve as a unique riser in a vignette. This one elevates an apothecary jar, but you'll find scales in lots of settings throughout this book. If you love a piece, you'll find a way to incorporate it in your decor again and again.

signature spaces

There are places in every home that feature larger items that you can't move from place to place—the cabinets you love, the kitchen table you gather around, your front porch or entry, or a stairway bannister. Because they're special spots in most homes, it's important to spruce them up and enjoy changing looks from time to time to keep things warm and inviting.

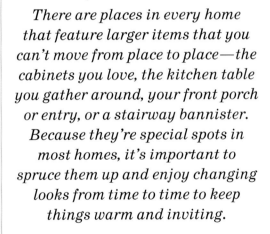

⌃ This teapot (sans lid) was a find I couldn't pass up. My great grandma, who lived to the age of 101, was named Lily. She grew lily of the valley alongside our house, and I've planted some alongside my home as well.

A kitchen table is at the heart of many homes. It's where memories are made and stories are shared. As a child, and later as a mom with my own kids, it's a spot that holds fond memories of the nearest and dearest people in my life. That's why I make a point of creating an inviting setting on our kitchen table year-round. It makes the place I love the most an important part of the decor.

Creating a vignette off to one end of the table is not only a design decision, but a practical one as well. It means two or three place settings can be set up on the opposite end of the table without having to dismantle the display. (And, keeping it real, we often plate our dinner from the stove to avoid having to clean up lots of serving dishes and give me more room to decorate.)

A rumpled runner sits beneath a vintage scale that creates a high/low look. If you're a dish collector like me, don't hide your dishes. Show them off in stacks, adding in some greenery, moss, or a little faux bird's nest for a hint of spring.

Before we dive further into this series of tabletops, I'll share that I'm at the stage in life where I no longer have small children at home. Our two daughters are grown and mostly away from the house. My husband and I often pull up a stool at the kitchen island to grab a quick bite to eat. When we do sit around our family table, it's more often set for two or three of us. But the table is adjacent to the island and kitchen, and it is definitely a focal point set right in front of

glass doors that open onto our backyard deck. So it's an eye-catching area.

When I want a more traditional setup, I still aim for a few unexpected elements to add interest. Turning a table runner sideways and gathering each draping end with a ribbon keeps the ends of the table open for serving pieces or a couple of additional place settings. If you're the type of collector who's got plate chargers or specialty dishes that you're saving for a special occasion, consider this your permission slip to make *every* day special. Stop waiting for "someday" to use them. Pull them out and delight your family with them today.

I opted to use a vintage sifter as a tray to corral the centerpiece items. The see-through screen isn't practical for lifting the entire look, but I'm able to slide it to one end if needed, and the screen allows the texture of the runner to be seen, which I love.

Moving pieces of my collections around the house is always satisfying. A couple of jars from my button collection, with one serving as a vase for faux flowers, add lots of visual interest without the weightiness that dense, solid-colored vases would.

As you peruse these pages, you'll notice throughout the book that I reuse, repurpose, and recycle many of my finds. I hope that inspires you to do the same. When a shopkeeper or vendor

asks me what I'm going to do with an item, I say "use it!" And I mean it. I don't always have a plan for things when I buy them, but I do know that everything is adaptable. I'll reimagine where and how to use it. Doing so keeps the looks fresh and allows me more fun with fewer rules to follow. I don't have to save that one special spot for an item to go in once a year. If you have items you love that have fallen under that spell, break the mold and use them elsewhere in your decor. It'll unlock lots of new possibilities!

The everyday look here features the sifter as a tray again but adds an open wire basket that provides lots of visual bang with its scalloped edge and airy appearance. A tarnished silver urn gives a lift to a spray of delicate twigs and ferns. A few stacks of assorted ironstone dishes mix well with some wood bowls and wood-handled kitchen tools in the pitcher. An angled runner beneath it all keeps the feeling casual and if we tug it a little to the right, there's still room for the hubs and me to have a quick bite to eat at the opposite end of the table.

Just off to the side of the sliding glass doors next to the table is a corner I love to spruce up with a same-but-different look using a tall pillar as a base for a fun display. As you turn the pages, you'll see a variety of items perched here.

Themed displays can be a delightful interruption to the ordinary. Can you imagine setting a table with this look for your book club or a fall festival evening with friends? I'm ready to pour myself a

⌃ *Layer, layer, layer! If you see a look you love, step in closer to see what's really happening. It might be the layers of texture, shape, and subtle colors that speak to your heart.*

cup of hot cider with a cinnamon stick stirrer and chat about the latest bestseller!

If you're looking for a place to begin collecting, you can't go wrong with vintage books. They are generally plentiful in antique shops and relatively easy to find at reasonable prices. I use them open, shut, spines facing out, spines facing in, nested in baskets, perched on open drawers, and more. Here, books take the place of a traditional fabric runner. If you can't get your stacks level enough to add subsequent layers, tuck a coaster in here or there to even things out.

Candles set a mood that makes a space more intimate. Using a mix of metal and ceramic holders in varying heights helps keep the eye moving across the table.

With the books and candles in place, the next step is tucking in the plants, pumpkins, and natural wood elements. The deep red pumpkins were a nursery gift shop find that add an appealing element of drama. A few white pumpkins atop short wood posts wrapped with jute twine bows accessorize the look.

At one end of the table, a small vintage suitcase is stacked with a platter, plates, and a vase. This could be where guest plates and silverware awaits partygoers on the night of an event. Or you could place a tureen of steaming hot cider with a ladle there for guests to fill their own mugs.

One last thing: even if you're not going to be sitting around the table, a pair of well-placed throw pillows adds to the ambience and cozies up the luxe look.

⌃ *The elegant penmanship on handwritten letters is an art form I fear we are losing. I keep it alive by collecting old letters and postcards. It's fun to display them by wrapping a few with a ribbon as if they're a stack of love letters. I do love them!*

It may seem counterintuitive, but as the holiday hustle and bustle ramps up, I try to keep things simple at the kitchen table. That's because I know we'll have guests popping in for meals, cards to write, and gifts to wrap. To that end, I try to contain the decor to a centerpiece that's easy to lift out of the way when needed.

Here a long, vintage, window box segment is the vessel for my mini forest of bottlebrush trees, but any long, shallow container would work. Adding a mix of matte and shiny silver ornaments adds a hint of sparkle. A few sprigs of greenery spilling over the edges complete the setting.

Once the holidays have passed, I'll swap out the ornaments for pine cones and the centerpiece can stay through January. 🎄

⌃ *The tall pillar, frame, and chair are almost always part of this corner decor. A few extra pieces are added to highlight the season or theme of the kitchen table setting.*

Call it what you will—a cupboard, a hutch, a china cabinet—I love, love, love everything about this type of furniture, especially if it has doors. In my mind, those doors are like the curtains in a theater. Sometimes you can fling the doors open wide and the shelves are your stage. Other times, you might get a peek at the stage behind one of the curtains. Or maybe they're both closed, but the doors are glass, so it's as if you're looking at a window display at the greatest store you can imagine, showcasing all of your treasures.

If you have a signature cabinet in your home, I encourage you to place it where you maintain all your door options. Is there space to leave one or both doors open? If yes, you've found the right spot.

The black-and-white items featured in the cupboard opposite include many small items. For that reason, I wanted the doors wide open so the little pieces didn't get lost behind them. I built the display by inserting the largest pieces first and then decorated with the smallest pieces. Because I wanted to play off all of the round clock faces, I centered a big round tin on the middle shelf to interrupt the flow. It causes your eye to move around the shelves in a circular fashion.

One trick I didn't use here was to add a vintage linen or textured piece draped over an open door to soften the look. If you're creating a wintry, warm, and cozy look, consider that option.

Closing one of the doors on the hutch creates a different decorating opportunity. I'm able to open

⌃ *Assorted black-and-white pieces hold together in a timeless, always-in-season approach to decorating, even when combining seemingly disparate items.*

a drawer beneath the closed door a bit and tuck in a cast iron element to break the lines of the door.

In this vignette, several large elements such as the corbel, the books, and the pair of antique white footstools hold their visual weight behind the glass door and don't require an up-close look to discern their natures. Smaller items and those with more delicate features, such as the ruffled edges on the stack of plates or the chippy paint and ridges of an architectural element, have finer details that are better showcased with the door open.

Look at the collection of items you've gathered as you're building your display to discern the best position for your cabinet doors and don't be afraid to change the door positions often. Shopping my own stash of collections as I redecorate reminds me of all the fun treasures I own and helps remind me what I want to be on the hunt for next time I'm out antiquing or thrifting.

Keep the interior color of your cabinet in mind as you're planning how to fill it. If the interior is a warm- or dark-tone wood, using lighter-tone items

⌃ *Footstools don't have to sit on the floor. Elevate their status by placing them on cupboard shelves and stacking them to show off their details in the legs or decorative edgings.*

will help them pop off the background. When the doors are open, usually the more I can fit into a display the better. But simple and minimal works too, especially with both doors closed.

Inspired by the bowling pins and little skittle pins and their touches of red, I brought in a vintage crocheted doily with red edging to drape from the center shelf. From there, I kept to big, chunky elements that would still read well with the doors shut.

The exterior of the cabinet presented a few more places to decorate. This time I used the small piece of real estate in front of the cabinet door to perch a basil plant and a few skittle pins. On top, I tipped a sugar mold on its side to repeat the circular shape you see on the scale and with the cloche and croquet ball. Succeeding in getting a look you love is partly learning to repeat an idea three (or five) times. That repetition creates a comforting effect. 🌱

« Faded colors can sometimes be more interesting than bright original paint. The soft tones speak to the timeworn affection and use many of these items have undergone.

" This cabinet is one of my favorites because of its chippy, untouched, aged exterior patina and the dark, warm, rustic interior. The contrast catches my eye. "

just the right angle

Almost nothing in a home is as immovable as a staircase. But that doesn't mean you're stuck with a ho-hum spot. Rather, it means that whether you have a sweeping staircase, a straight staircase, or a split staircase with a landing like I do, you can work to make it something special. Who wants a permanent fixture in their home that lacks style? Not me!

My staircase has an open railing up to the landing, which gives me the opportunity to treat the space in front of the railing and the stairwell wall as one cohesive area. Here, I began with a set of auditorium seats in the foreground with a couple of pretty cushions added for comfort. The metal piece with horizontal bars behind the right-hand seat is a salvage railing piece, but I turned it on end to use it as a vintage book rack to show off a couple books with interesting covers and an old cane.

On the stairwell wall, I began with five antique paintbrushes from my collection. I encircled them with an ornate but empty picture frame, keeping its twisty wire visible. To fill the space, I surrounded the frame with a variety of similarly toned elements, keeping the top of the display mostly straight (until the ceiling soffit budges in) and added items to the row of hooks that gradually step down to mimic the angle of the stairs.

When you take in the entire area, I hope it feels inviting enough that you'd like to linger here with a good book! It does to me.

A gorgeous antique Lonestar quilt with the colors of late summer and early fall is the seasonal focal point and the inspiration for all the additional elements I pulled into the area. Perched on the auditorium seats are a pair of vintage metal picnic baskets, as well as a few heirloom gourds whose soft colors are perfectly pale. An old sifter rests on a ledge behind the right-hand seat supporting a wreath whose round shape repeats the ring around the quilt's center star.

Keeping it simple on the stairwell wall, a pair of vintage scissors is a nod to the quiltmaker and two handmade brooms are perfectly placed for the long and short sides of the wall, adding balance. If you're paying attention to the littlest details, note that the cane from the paintbrush setting on page 121 is now a quilt holder.

⌃ Seasonal touches that add texture without too much color like these braided raffia ears of corn are always on my "must buy" list. They'll find their way into my decor for years to come.

> *Get creative with stairwell walls to keep the look balanced. Same-but-different items, like these two brooms, help prevent a lopsided appearance.*

How many sleeps 'til Christmas? At the holidays, you can wrap everything in greenery and color me happy. There's nothing this Minnesota gal loves better than bringing the outdoors in. I use a mix of real and faux so I can extend the season and not worry about too many needles dropping here and there.

I'm also happy to add a pop of color to an earth-toned setting by giving my jolly red Santa a special spot and filling his sleigh with some of the red ornaments from my Shiny Brites collection. A trio of glittery gold bottlebrush trees add a little luxe as they mirror the metallic baubles swagging from a ribbon garland on the stair rail.

And good swag is important, so I absolutely go off-center with my stair-rail garland. It eliminates obsessing over whether it's just right and evenly balanced. Instead, I'm able to tie it up in a jiffy with silk ribbons and not give it another thought.

Adding a sprig of greenery to the Christmas Tree Farm paper scroll on the back wall along with an additional swag of ornament garland ties the foreground and background together. I'm hiding a few Christmas morning surprises in those vintage suitcases below the bench. Shhhh, don't tell.

⌃ Treat your stair rail like an extra wall and hang a favorite framed piece on it! Thread a ribbon through the hanger and tie it securely to a couple of posts. If it wobbles too much, a bit of clay (used to keep picture frame corners from slipping on the wall) placed on the back of the frame where it touches the rail should do the trick.

⌃ The open rails that run across the length of the shelves were likely great for holding shoes at the factory, but I have to get creative when it comes to stacking my favorite pieces atop the shelves so everything stays level.

Do you have any absolutes? Certain objects or items you don't care for in home decor or colors you don't use in your decorating? I think we all do. Mine is blue. I don't care for the color blue, so I rarely wear it or decorate with it. Until I do. Until something comes along like these amazing blueware bowls and yellowware bowls with blue stripes, and then all of sudden, I'm absolutely in love!

This is to say, you never know when you start antiquing or collecting what is going to speak to your heart. And if you fall in love with something you don't normally care for, take a chance on it. Something unexpectedly beautiful might just emerge.

My vintage factory shoe cart with caster wheels is a favorite piece. Its mix of rusty metal and rustic wood rails offers plenty of space to play with my wares to make an artful display. Some people put glass shelves on carts like these, as the open rails make it more challenging to decorate. But I embrace both the openness and the challenge.

This beauty in blue was a summertime setup, so I incorporated a vintage catcher's mitt and some softballs, indigo wrapped yarn balls, and classic baseballs. Books, folded ticking fabric, plates, and upside-down bowls work as risers and levelers to hold other treasure and prevent pieces from slipping through the slats. Is it more work than just slipping in a wood or glass shelf insert? Yes,

but keeping the overall airy look of the cart is more important to me, so I make accommodations.

One of the things I love most about my bowl collections is the variety of ways to display them. They nest well. I can flip one upside down as a base for another. And perhaps best of all, they serve as vessels to be filled with other favorite finds and collected items.

And if you're wondering why the two plump pillows on the base shelf of the cart are there, know that I'm keeping it real. I'm the proud momma to five cats and these pillows provide a perfect spot for my purrfect little friends to curl up for a nap.

I may not turn over an entirely new leaf when it comes to my favorite colors to live with and wear, but I believe this hint of blue in our home decor is a blue-ribbon idea that's going to stick around for a while.

66

Summertime and the living should be easy. Playful looks and breezy colors can set a feeling that blurs the lines between indoors and out.

99

Collecting is a process that happens over time and something you can't rush if you want to enjoy the thrill of the hunt. But I'm a big believer in living with what you love and surrounding yourself with things that give you joy and energy. There's no point in collecting if you're storing everything away and saving it for "someday." So here's a tip if you're just starting out and you've found your favorite first bowl and are still hunting for a second or third one:

Find a lidded basket that's a bit longer and wider than the base of your bowl. Prop the lid open and nestle your bowl inside. In the space that's left, add a potted plant for a pop of green. If you find a second smaller bowl, you can nest it in the first one. Or fill your bowl with another item or two that you treasure!

This cart arrangement brings me back to my neutral comfort zone with a look that blends seamlessly with my everyday decor. If there is a theme, it's about the right materials and textures setting the tone for the room they're in. Ribbed ceramic pots, natural and wood-tone woven baskets, rusted metals, earthenware jugs, and creamy accents are gathered for a vignette that I can enjoy daily.

The lower shelf includes a double stack of small suitcases that fit the cart to a tee. As a foil to their straight lines, I added a low wooden bowl and round ceramic pot to balance the look. On the shelf just above, I placed a basket I found at Target that seems like it was custom-made for this cart. Fitting the basket on the shelf allowed me to fill in with more small items than usual, such as a porch spindle and little crock, without having to concern myself with things falling through the shelf rails.

Notice that the woven basket element is repeated two more times, with a market basket on the top shelf and a fishing creel draped over one end. Not only does this fit the design rule of thumb that three repeating elements are pleasing; but it also forms a more organic design with the fishing basket breaking across the lines of the shelf frame. The iron stand on the left and large fern on top serve the same role, softening the boxiness of the shoe rack.

Many of these items reappear in other rooms in my house from time to time. That's because I live with what I love and try to move things around as I decorate, rather than store them out of sight.

⌃ *Think about angles as you build a shelf display. Not everything has to align squarely. Turning some things askew or tilting them as I did with the books and a pot adds casual interest and keeps the eye moving.*

When fall arrives, it's time to warm up my decor with the season's bounty. Five white locker baskets were the starting point for this shelf arrangement. They're perfect for filling with assorted items without blocking the view of what's inside. And my trusty shelf-size woven basket helps corral the goodies on the bottom shelf.

A trip to the pumpkin patch is a treat I still enjoy and the variety of shapes and colors available each year seems to multiply. So, I set out to fill my wagon with white pumpkins in a variety of shapes. Three large ones perch on a few favorite pottery pieces. To elevate the top pumpkin to the height I wanted, I turned a small bowl upside down inside the largest yellow bowl, and nested the medium bowl atop it. Voilà! Problem solved.

From there I picked a grouping of like items to fill each locker basket: white mini pumpkins in one, wood mashers and kitchen tools in another, and amber glass bottles and jugs and stoneware in the remaining basket. Stacking some items on their sides and others upright helps showcase their shapes and add variety. Tucking in a few hints of orange adds a surprise pop of color that highlights, but doesn't overwhelm, the fall theme.

Overall, I enjoy the contrast between the baskets that you can see through and the visually dense bowls and jugs. The mix allows the patterns in the bowls to shine too. The finished look makes me want to head back out to the pumpkin patch for a cup of hot cider and an apple donut. 🌼

armoire affection

M uch like the scratch-and-dent section of your local appliance store, you can often buy a vintage furniture piece for a song if it's in less-than-ideal condition. For example, this small armoire was missing the front panel on the door. Maybe it once held a mirror that broke. Who knows? Regardless, the price was absolutely right to make the piece mine. I treat it as a small cupboard and pretend there's still a piece of glass in front of those little shelves.

On white furniture with a light interior, dark colors create drama so I shopped my home to gather clockfaces, picnic baskets, and all the browns and tans I could find to create a rich display.

> 66
>
> *As you walk through your house and its rooms, recognize that it is more than just a house. It's a home that you fill with the people and things you love most.*
>
> 99

⌃ *Twist, tuck, and turn items in your displays to add layer upon layer of interest. What holds this group of random goods together is the homogenous color palette.*

When I was ready to rearrange the armoire, I kept a few pieces from the fall-feeling cabinet (the big star and some pottery), but wanted a lighter, cleaner look that wasn't as visually weighty. I also wanted to use the door frame (remember there's no glass in it) as a decor element, so I flung it open wide and draped it with a vintage linen tablecloth with a fancy tatted edging I adore.

Building from the bottom up, a graduated stack of platters fills one shelf (see the caption at right for my secret to filling the space with just six platters). Adding a rattan tray beneath the dishware was an afterthought once I chose the large basket for the center shelf. Placing the tray under the platters doesn't take much space, but it helps to repeat the woven basket texture.

From there a mixture of pairs—mini loving cups, wicker-wrapped bottles, mortars and pestles, and cigar boxes—round out the bulk of the display for a calm and classic feeling.

⌃ *On an open space, such as a coffee table or a kitchen island, a stack of platters creates concentric drama on its own. But inside a cabinet, subtle differences in shapes can be lost. Adding spacers (such as the upside down bowls shown here) between platters makes sure each one has a chance to shine.*

> *You don't need a degree in interior design to decorate your home. Just be passionate about seeing how others create the looks you love and adapt those ideas for your spaces.*

If there are sprouts from little flower bulbs peeking up through the snow in the garden beds, I'm inside declaring that spring has sprung! And that means pulling out pastel McCoy pottery pieces, ironstone platters, floral prints, faux tulips, little floral sprays, and small plants that look as if they might be starts from the greenhouse. It may be weeks before the snow is gone for good, but indoors things are springing to life.

An airy look in the spring feels easy and breezy, so it's the time of year I pare down some of the layering and leave a bit more breathing room. If you haven't got a green thumb, that doesn't mean you can't be a collector of beautiful vintage ceramic pots. Stack them, upend them, nest them, and perch them. Artificial or real, if you choose to add a few plants, find little ones that hint at the plethora of green that will soon cover the trees and lawns but aren't quite revealed yet. Spring is a season of anticipation. 🌸

⌃ Manufactured in the early 20th century, McCoy pottery was made in many colors. I'm partial to the pinks, greens, and burgundies. McCoy Pottery is known (and adored) for its attention to detailing.

> ❝
> *If pastel colors speak to your heart in everyday decor,*
> *this setting could be made less springlike by removing the tulips*
> *and adding in a few cream pottery pieces.*
> ❞

ARMOIRE AFFECTION

↟ *While faux bird eggs make sense with the setup, the thread cards may seem like a bit of a stretch. But don't be too literal with what you include. If the colors and tones are right, you can make it work!*

"
Give your family room a well-deserved upgrade with an arrangement on your coffee table that's exciting and inviting.
"

The humble coffee table can hold a beverage or bowl of popcorn, or it can hold a stack of coffee table books on a tray with a scented candle. Neither is wrong, but it can also do oh-so-much-more. I invite you to think of your coffee table as the center of attention in your great room, living room, or family room. Let it be a spot where you celebrate a season, showcase your fabulous finds, and enjoy sharing your wares. Yes, there's still room to set down your coffee cup or phone, but let's agree to banish boring or expected when it comes to coffee tables.

First off, can we offer thanks that the console television has gone away? That means that in most rooms that have a television, they are usually on the wall or atop a stand. Why is this important? Because it's nice to have some height in your coffee table decor but your family won't have to peer through it to watch their favorite TV shows. Crisis averted.

I do like to begin with a tray or base of some sort so that I can slide the arrangement in one direction or another if need be. The metal-and-wood garden caddy is a staple piece I use often. Here, it's part of a garden-themed arrangement paired with an ornamental birdhouse. The pots, plants and extra pieces are purposefully askew, so they won't have to be tidied up too often. And the view you see is from a chair across the room. Now isn't that fun?

The layered look is a go-to in my home decor. This stack includes a sifter basket base (the same one used in the gardening/birdhouse coffee table display on page 141), a wire commercial bread basket, dough bowl, and vintage crochet thread balls in assorted sizes. This top-down look gives you an idea of how to stagger layered elements to add interest. It also shows how adding a handful of extra items can instantly turn an everyday display into a seasonal one.

A few holiday ornaments, some rolled sheet music, sprigs of greenery, pine cones, and dark porch post pieces add a festive touch to celebrate the season. After the holidays, the ornaments can be packed away, and the centerpiece will hold through the first weeks of the new year.

But as February approaches, it's fun to refresh the look by replacing the dark porch posts with lighter architectural pieces. Vintage Valentine candy boxes will replace the pine cones and sheet music, and a couple of playful Xs and Os will sit alongside an antique heart-shaped cookie cutter. I love to collect vintage ephemera and children's valentine cards are a favorite category, so I tuck in some of them for a pop of color and whimsy. Using this build-up-from-the-base approach simplifies the changeover between seasons. In addition, it means if you find the perfect size of layering pieces for your table, you've got the framework set to build your vision. That's a win in my book.

Think of seasonal decorating like accessorizing a favorite outfit. Keep the foundation of a look you love and change a few embellishments.

Can't you just picture this toolbox filled with silver-plated champagne buckets and vintage loving cups topped with frosted white bottlebrush trees for a January display?

But, of course, I find joy in mixing things up more than keeping them the same, so the base elements on my coffee table don't stay out for more than a few months without wholesale changes.

In the fall, I love to change all the decor to make it warm and cozy. A vintage carpenter's toolbox (page 144) opens up to display an abundance of fall goodies, including dried cornstalk leaves, a carnival game spinner (that color, swoon!), pumpkins, gourds, pine cones (they're not just for winter!), and a linen throw with its knotted edge spilling out for a bit of softness. If you don't have pets or small children at home, bittersweet branches are a beautiful addition to add a little burst of orange. (I included them here for the photo but removed them right after because bittersweet is toxic to cats.) 🐱

>> *A champagne crate is the "tray" that corrals my dark-and-light display. I love the juxtaposition and contrast of colors, values, and shapes. What looks like a dried seed head in the vase is actually a cut flower. Try breaking apart a grocery-store bouquet to showcase your favorite blooms.*

small places

Maybe you live in a small space without room for big furniture. Or perhaps you haven't yet moved into your dream home to realize all your big decor ideas. Don't let space limitations scale down your style. There are plenty of ways to create stunning vignettes in the smallest of spaces. Living with one-of-a-kind finds you treasure nourishes the soul.

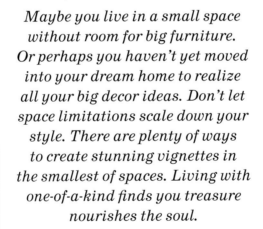

top drawer decor

E legant and graceful are words that describe swans, as well as the feeling I was going for with this vignette. When you enter the front door of our home, you can see all the way through to the back wall of the house. This hairpin-leg table is on that back wall that you see first, opposite the front door. Because it's in such an attention-grabbing position, I try to make sure it has an equally eye-catching display each season.

Though it's narrow and not too deep, this leggy table is about the height of a sofa table, commanding attention and allowing me to decorate below it as well as on top. (If it were end-table height, it might appear too wimpy from eight or ten yards away.)

The cement swan planter on the floor anchors the bottom of the arrangement, while a large mesh arch and frame take the top of the display nearly to the ceiling for added drama. A tall cloche on a low pedestal connects the elements by breaking into the frame above it. Keeping things mostly monochromatic adds to the serenity of the setting.

⌃ *Propped upright in open drawers, shells and coral are right at home alongside the swans, amplifying the water theme and bringing depth and texture to the display.*

> Sometimes you have to take chances. I bought this painting online, hoping the colors were true. When it arrived, I was thrilled to see that its colors matched my pottery pieces perfectly.

An oil painting of irises and carnations that I found online inspired me to pull my pink, burgundy, and cream McCoy pottery vases out of storage and into this springlike setting. As you build your collections, try to keep in mind your favorite color palettes so that when an opportunity presents itself you can visualize how other pieces you own may coordinate. Knowing I had pottery in these same colors, a plan started to percolate in my head.

Once the picture was hung at eye level, I needed height so my decor items would intersect the bottom edge of the painting, connecting all the elements. The miniature green shelf is the perfect shade to anchor the left side of the look. Opposite it, a pedestal and tall cloche encasing a deep green seltzer bottle balance out the tabletop. I tucked in McCoy pottery pieces on the shelf, beneath the cloche, on the table, and in the drawers, taking care to keep the colors distributed in a fashion similar to the floral painting.

To fill the space between the shelf and the cloche, I went back to a reliable trick—a stack of books and a few tipped pots. A handful of flower frogs and figurines complete the look.

⌃ *Mixed metals, chippy wood, classic pottery, and dried florals blend well together beneath a tall cloche, adding just the right mix of colors to balance the vibrant oil painting.*

> Timeless appeal. One-of-a-kind character. A warm and comfy feel that's like a hug for your home. That's the vibe I want in the fall.

Much like Mother Nature in autumn, time lends each vintage piece its own patina. The antique suitcases tell a story of travels far and wide, of places seen, and people met. With all of the small drawers closed, the table takes on a more subdued role in this display with a more uniform look than some of my other displays.

Here, the larger elements take most of the focus, with fewer small bits and bobs. It's not my go-to look (usually I'm all about the bits and bobs!), but when it works, there's an understated elegance that is both calming and inviting.

A small drawered box on the left has more drawers missing from its cubbies than not, but I made the most of the drawers it does have to hold old glass bottles, pheasant feathers, and mini pumpkins. A mottled black urn on top is in keeping with the rustic feeling, and the filler of bare twigs and faded fern stems is a nod to the season ahead. The muted, soft tones of the larger pumpkins enable this look to linger from September through November.

If the edges of all the hard pieces feel too austere, you could soften a look like this by placing a vintage linen tablecloth or soft throw atop the table prior to adding the other elements.

⌃ *Never pass up an interesting porch post piece. The detailing is delightful. And they can serve as pumpkin perches or be tipped over for a low-profile, rustic sensibility.*

⌃ *An antique tinsel tree topper extends beyond the edge of the window frame to add shape to the "tree." Mini linen grainsack stockings layer on even more texture and interest.*

In an open concept living arrangement, it's difficult not to have areas competing for attention as you look around the room, especially during the holidays. And much like a great show on Broadway, a good supporting cast is essential. I'm all about the Christmas tree being the center of attention, so I purposefully turn down the volume on other settings in the room.

Because this table is placed against the wall you see from our front door, I'm interested in a look that captures your attention from afar rather than it shouting, "Here I am!" To that end, I began with the simplest of tree shapes formed on the muntins of an antique window frame. Fresh-cut cedar branches are wired on in a primitive manner. A vintage star-shaped tree topper caps off the window.

To connect the tree frame with the table below, I filled a tall, golden funeral basket with sparse branches. I repeated the feel of the window frame by adding an ornate vintage frame and a cream-framed mirror leaning against the wall. A champagne bucket houses a tiny live tree with gold baubles. And the look finishes with a basket of pine cones and greenery nestled below the table. Eye-catching? Yes! Overwhelming? No! ❄

⌃ *Don't overlook adding the little extras. Tiny birds frosted with glitter adorn the branches as a surprise element when you step in for a closer look.*

filled with delight

A shelf of cubbies is akin to a jewelry box for your vintage cache, a chance to give each of your finds its due. And while many cubby displays show several pieces of a single collection, don't overlook the chance to show a variety of objects of a common hue rather than like objects. Have you met a collector who only collects blue and white, regardless of what the object is? Your palette might not be as limited, but you can sort your treasures by color palette and build a look to suit the seasonal or everyday vibe you're after. Cream to brown and several shades in between hold together a disparate group of objects in style. Think of it as your recipe for success!

Have you ever tossed more veggies into a bowl of tuna salad you were making to bulk up the amount you'd have for sandwiches? Or maybe you've stretched a breakfast casserole by adding in some extra hashbrowns or some diced ham? Starting out as collector, you can think of stretching your finds with a few "fillers" in the same way you do in the kitchen.

The cubbies on page 159 mostly showcase collections of ironstone creamers and butter pat plates. Rather than leaving empty spaces once I exhausted pieces from my collection, I took a cue from the little plates to introduce a few filler pieces that complemented the look. The intricate details of the butter pats mimicked some of the artwork on vintage needle packs and small pharmaceutical bottles. Adding these elements filled in the gaps and completed the display.

Do you prefer cubbies that are uniform in size with every opening the same, or cubbies that are a bit irregular with openings that vary? I have both types, but in my heart, there is a soft spot for those that are more dissimilar than similar in shape. That helps when I encounter a printer drawer shelf like this where it's likely that some of the original dividers are missing and spaces vary in width by horizontal and vertical rows.

What appeals to me about irregularities are the opportunities to display objects of differing sizes and shapes. From a delicate vintage needle pack to a chunky little ironstone creamer, there's a spot that's just perfect to show off just about everything!

If you're concerned about stability or the odd angles of a piece like this versus the fragility of the items placed inside, a little bit of museum wax (usually found near picture-hanging supplies in the hardware store) goes a long way to ease the nerves. It prevents an errant bump from turning into broken bits of china. Simple as that!

⌃ *If your cubbies are deep and dark, try to situate the items you're placing inside toward the front edge to prevent them from being too darkened by shadows.*

57 BUTTERMILK ACRES

One of my favorite features of this cubby shelf is its mesh backing. It allows so much light into the back, preventing each cubby from being a dark little hole. Placed against a light wall, it appears to highlight each of the treasures it holds.

The Jewel T spice tins were the impetus for the entire arrangement. When I came across them while antiquing, I bought the whole lot at the same time because I'd never seen spice tins in this colorway. As a collector, my best advice to you is if you see something unusual that you love, buy it if you can. It's rare to come across an instant collection, but I use distressed, faded colors for fall, so I knew they'd blend in with things I already owned. French pudding cups, nutmeg brown stoneware, mustard jars, brass candlesticks, a bundle of natural tallow berries, and mini pitchers and bottles fill out the vignette I fall for every time I round the corner. 🌿

» The typography of classic logos and fonts is always interesting. When you find an object with text that has survived through decades without becoming too chipped or worn, it's a keeper!

get the corner on style

Are you a fan of changing your decor and style frequently throughout your home? I am, for sure. But there's one area of our home that has a more consistent look from season to season. Why is that? It's a very small space. If you have a similar situation, once you find a look you love, why not keep a few basic pieces in that area so you don't have to conquer the same difficulties repeatedly?

In our house, the corner near our family dinner table is next to a sliding glass door that leads to the deck. There are lots of ins and outs in the summer to take food to the grill and drinks outdoors, so anything too fussy in that area is out. My solution has been to keep a sturdy porch pillar in the corner, a large frame on the wall, and a favorite chippy chair in that spot. With those three staple items as a base, I mix and match a few smaller pieces to suit the seasons. And best of all, I've eliminated the search for what will fit in that space. Win-win! ✣

side table swagger

Call it what you will, the side or end table has suffered too long in the home-dec wasteland as a place that holds a lamp and two coasters. It's time to reclaim this stellar spot as a supporting player for clever decor. If the coffee table is the star, then we've got to make sure the end table isn't the never-to-be-seen understudy.

STARTING POINT

What does it take to replicate this sweet bundle of books that would work easily as well tucked into a shelf display? Two vintage books in your choice of color, a small strip cut from a tattered old quilt, a bit of twine, and a vintage charm is all you need. It's a little investment for a grand look your friends will admire.

Natural light from windows, floor lighting, and overhead ceiling lighting provide lots of options for keeping you out of the dark. So perhaps you don't need lamps on your end tables to make them sparkle. This one is located between a pair of chairs in our family room. I use suitcases in our home year-round. Here a pair are stacked with the top one open to hold a vintage vase and a pair of old paintbrushes. To get a third paintbrush in the mix, I had what I think was a stroke of genius and used an old clipboard to highlight a green-handled brush. A trio of smaller brushes rests in front of it.

Because I wanted a spring look, I chose green as my pop of color and included a pair of green books and a fern leaf. The bowls and bottle balance the look and bring it to the front edge of the table, but they're also easily moved when someone wants to set down a drink or snack.

Seasonal fun is another delightful use for the seldom celebrated side table. Maybe you don't want to go wild changing things up for a short celebration season, but even a shoebox or two of Halloween collectibles can be frightfully adorable when displayed together.

An array of new finds mixed with vintage favorites is on display here. I'll let you decide what's old and what's new, because, frankly, there are some fabulous remakes available in the Halloween realm these days. And I've no problem (nor should you) comingling the old with the new.

You might recognize the little white chest from other displays in the book, but here it's gone to good use with the top being the highest perch for a jack-o-lantern. One of the chest's drawers serves double duty as a ledge for a box of "cooky" cutters. My favorite find, though, was a full set of upper- and lowercase alphabet stamps which I pulled from to spell the word *pumpkins* in tiny letters across the base of the table. If it's oversized or undersized it has my heart. Cheers to a tiny pumpkin victory! 🎃

FINISHING TOUCHES

If you're a fan of typography like me, then be on the lookout for items with letters, such as stamps, stencils, handwriting teaching sets, blocks, and game pieces. Numbers are fun to collect too, to denote special days of the month, years, anniversaries, and birthdays. Collect them both and incorporate them in multiple ways throughout the year.

Keep in mind that you don't have to pass up incomplete letter and number sets either. Mixing and matching assorted pieces to spell a word or signify a date can be equally eye-catching in its presentation.

> " It's possible to allude to hobbies you love without showing the fruits of your labor. I love hand embroidery and this display highlights some vintage tools of the trade. "

believe in second chances

Sewing notions and bits of nature mix well on this mug rack showcasing a collection of old bobbins, thread spools, and more. Don't worry about being too literal as you gather your wares. A carpenter's folding ruler isn't a sewing implement, but it alludes to a measuring tape.

Fern branches add three pops of green. I especially like the spool at the top turned on its side with a fern coming out of one end, adding a touch of whimsy. The pair of wooden bowls slip behind the pegs to hold them upright and help break up the straight lines of the wooden bobbins and spools. Plus, they mirror some wooden bowls used in the "Everyday Ease" kitchen look (see page 79) that's adjacent to this mug rack. (Again, carrying a decor theme between areas in our home.)

Crochet thread balls are used as a neutral filler. I prefer catching them on the tips of the pegs so that they don't align perfectly. Having them askew makes a more interesting overall effect.

On the bottom ledge, old thread bobbins are piled in various groups to tie back into the fibers used above and to soften the look.

⌃ *Don't pass up an item because a chunk of it is missing or imperfect. Those are the real-life worn elements that add one-of-a-kind interest when you're up close.*

To tell the truth, this mug rack is an example of a decor piece that I didn't really care for when I tried using it for its intended purpose. Filled with coffee mugs, it was visually dense and not very artful. However, as a display piece for items other than mugs, it's great!

There is so much potential in those pegs, the gaps between them, and the small ledges. Because I like to repeat a seasonal theme across several areas of our home, this wall decor complements the "Spring Awakening" mantel look on page 24. Clay pots and a mix of faux greenery mingle with small-scale gardening hand tools. Notice the variety of ways the pegs are used to corral, pierce, and suspend the pieces.

When you're adding elements to a display such as this, consider the path your eyes will move along the shape you create. It might be a Z, an S, an O, or a diagonal line. Regardless, stand back and make sure the arrangement leads your eye to move around. And don't forget the top edge of a frame. It can serve as another shelf or ledge and allow you to break across the straight lines of a frame or shelf. Here, a pair of checkered gardening gloves add some softness and a little pop of color.

⌃ Turn accidental breakage into a decorating opportunity. Artfully arranging the clay pot shards and tucking in bits of moss adds an organic touch.

> An orphan item, such as a pot lid or a single corbel, is often overlooked at antique shops or junk fairs. I prize them for their one-of-a-kind beauty.

One-of-a-kind finds suit my style perfectly, so I don't concern myself with having the matching base if a pot cover or lid dazzles me. But displaying these cuties, with their classic relief designs or graceful handles, can be a challenge. Plate hangers slipped over the mug rack pegs are the perfect solution to securely showcase this trio of lids.

The lower ledge is the perfect width to line up a few antique mashers, though I was careful to choose ones with thinner bases from my collection, so they'd sit between the pegs. I tucked a couple of ink bottles on the opposite side of the lower ledge, but it felt too predictable to place more on top of the mug rack. Rather, I turned the bottles upside down and hung them each on a peg, so they appear as if they're drying on a drying rack.

Because the wood tones of the mug rack frame and corbel are so similar, the rectangular shape of the frame becomes more artful and organic with the corbel atop it. The antique carved 1913 bread board and piece of driftwood repeat the wood tone twice more and a soft, chunky knit potholder hangs off the lower edge for a bit of softness.

⌃ *Casual yet sophisticated nooks that elevate the everyday make the ordinary extraordinary. What a lovely way to celebrate your home.*

The sweep and detailing the corbel adds to my rack earned it the right to stay in place as I swapped out some pieces for fall. At first glance, the crisp black accents pop off the light background and the mixture of warm wood tones play off cool white milk glass and ironstone. But when you take a closer look, you'll see there's more fun to be had than first meets the eye.

My favorite addition is not one but two mini paper cutters. For me, they hearken back to the school office where pages upon pages of papers and art supplies were trimmed. A little six-inch square cutter tucks behind two pegs perfectly. The second cutter is a bit more of a mystery, as it has no grid lines to help keep cuts straight. Its narrow width also mystifies me. Was it a receipt or postcard cutter? A little book trimmer? A custom piece? Who knows, but I love its unusual rectangular shape.

A couple of clipboards and a few favorite numbers round out the vignette. Paper leaves cut from newsprint flutter down with a subtle nod to the season. Happy fall!

⌃ *Every antique tells a story. The blade handle on the square paper cutter appears a bit ominous, but I'd guess at one time it had a softer handle cover that broke off, exposing the metal beneath.*

picture in picture

Fabulous finds that emerge when you least expect them are my favorite. This painting caught my eye when I was online window-shopping through some vintage sites. I was fascinated at first glance because of the background at the top of the painting. I think it's actually wallpaper that the artist painted on as the canvas.

In addition to the intrigue over the background, the colors in the painting also caught my attention because I knew I had a green watering can that would mimic the elegant green vase in the painting.

Setting up the display on my dining room sideboard, I replicated the roses from the picture with a single stem in a vase. The addition of the chippy metal birds, mini nest and egg, and tipped-over pot carries on the nature theme with same-but-different natural elements.

Creating similar vignettes in your home can be as simple as visualizing the grouping as a picture-in-picture display. Whether you coordinate the tones of the artwork, repeat elements of objects in the picture, or play off a favorite feature in the painting, it's a simple way to begin honing your decorating skills.

⌃ *Don't tuck away ephemera you find until you can afford to frame it. This vintage book page spread was not only the right color, but also had the spring vibe I was going for, so I tacked it on wall with a bit of adhesive wax and it's good to go!*

some looks
begin with color

Sometimes a vignette doesn't begin with a specific collection of items, but rather with color. The soft tones of the ombré vases launched this look and led me to gather other related spring-themed items to create a mood.

This setting was designed for those transitional days when some of us are yearning for spring, but the bright colors of new growth are still hibernating beneath a blanket of snow. I wasn't yet ready to go all out with tulips and daffodils, but I was ready to add a touch of lightness.

The cream tones of the vases coordinate with aged paper from books and a handwritten note on a vintage card. Ceramic and metal flower frogs add more greens and browns to the mix. Dried flowers and fresh sedum repeat the pinks and greens.

Chippy vintage frames with their old hanging wires still attached evoke a touch of rustic charm, mimicking the rusty metal drawers of the cabinet.

If you're just beginning to collect vintage furniture pieces, you can look for a multi-drawered piece like this to use as an end table or entryway piece. Propping open a couple of drawers and stacking books atop them to serve as an extra surface beyond the top of the chest allows for more variation in height and depth. (Also, consider giving a lift to pieces such as this, off the floor and onto a higher spot, as shown on page 12.)

Do you have a passion for making art or getting in touch with your crafting side? This lights-and-darks setup was an homage to those parts of my personality and lifestyle.

Collections of paintbrushes, crochet thread balls, and buttons reflect a playful approach in an everyday setting. The chicken waterer housing the thread balls and the little white chest it sits atop are pieces I use and reuse over and over. Keep that versatility in mind as you shop for items like these. Not wedding yourself to a piece aways living in a specific spot in your home opens up so many possibilities.

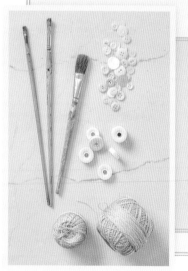

FINISHING TOUCHES

All the fillers used were selected on the basis of their color, which I kept purposefully light and neutral. Certainly they all share a crafty, creative-supply bent. But limiting the brush handles, buttons, and threads to creamy light ones adds a high degree of contrast against the dark base cabinet, resulting in a more dramatic look. Using elements in unexpected ways—a thread cone, a crochet ball, and a jar of buttons as a paintbrush holders—adds a dash of whimsy, a lightness of being!

"

Let's talk turkey! Sometimes a small display of seasonal decor to celebrate a special day is just what's needed to bring a smile to your guests' faces.

"

You have to be in a fowl mood to embrace a display like this, but who doesn't enjoy a little tomfoolery around Thanksgiving? Too much for you—or just right? If it's the latter, start searching for glazed ceramic pieces that celebrate Tom Turkey. Who knew they came in all shapes and sizes? Some of mine are old liquor bottles, creamers, salt and pepper shakers, lidded pots, and gravy boats. I've found both all-white pieces and colorful variations.

Want to know the spot where I've had the most success hunting for my turkeys? The thrift store! It seems these seasonal collectibles might not be the most treasured in some family collections, but you can gobble up the fun (and thrifty) finds with a plan like this in mind!

The drawers of the dark base unit again serve as shelves when pulled out one or two at a time. Having the option to open and close different drawers to create just the right spacing between pieces is a benefit of using this type of cabinet as a table. Adding a few elements on the floor in front of the cabinet ensures that the open bottom drawers aren't a trip hazard. A vintage scale on top and a dried seed pod complete the terrific look. 🦃

⌃ *Books level off the tops of open drawers, providing a place for pumpkins, gourds, and turkeys to rest.*

a behind-the-scenes vignette

I t seems as though we're all captivated with how things are made and love getting a behind-the-scenes peek at our favorite places or artisans in action. It fuels our imagination to visualize just what goes into the making of those special things we love.

Why not use that same imaginative spark when creating your own decor vignettes? That's what I did here.

Artisans inspire me. I imagined an artist's loft where space was at a premium. No room for an easel? I opted instead for a primitive bench turned work surface. An unframed, vintage canvas is propped up as though it's a work in progress.

Next, I gathered a collection of paintbrushes and a few small vessels capable of holding brushes or water for the artist to dip her brushes into.

Finally, I topped off the look with a single classic set of watercolor paints. I was fortunate to find an old, used set, but if I hadn't, I would've scuffed up and dabbled with a new set to give it the same well-worn look I love.

The result? A creative nook that looks as though the artist herself just stepped away from her work. Imagine the possibilities for creating your own behind-the-scenes artisan vignettes.

counting
your sheep

Often, budding collectors feel as if they need a dozen of something to "qualify" as a collector. I say, no way! Perhaps you have an interest in owls, or mid-century thermoses, or thistle motifs. They needn't all appear on the same type of object or be a of a similar scale. A collection of three to five items can still make a statement, even if they're not like one another.

An antique framed piece titled "The Two Flocks," featuring sheep on a hillside looking up at sheep in the clouds, inspired me to gather a few vintage lamb planters and figurines.

In surveying my finds, the gold highlights in the ears of the two lying-down sheep led me to include a trio of brass candlesticks to repeat the shiny elements of the ears and the frame itself. I paired a dark tin box with a book to raise the small frame and add height to the center of the display. Finishing the look were a few sprigs of greenery and moss, plus a few dark wood pieces that repeat the black in the framed artwork, to create a pastoral little scene. 🍃

The Two Flocks.

collections

Creating a home with one-of-a-kind character is the goal, but the thrill of the hunt for unique pieces is half the fun. The photos that follow are filled with pieces from my collections meant to inspire you on your journey to creating your own one-of-a-kind look. Choose your favorites, and even if our looks are different, gain insight on how to decorate your home with collections of things you love the most.

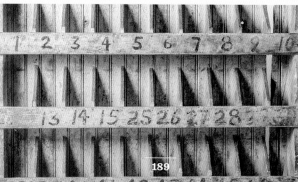
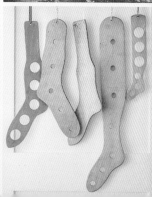

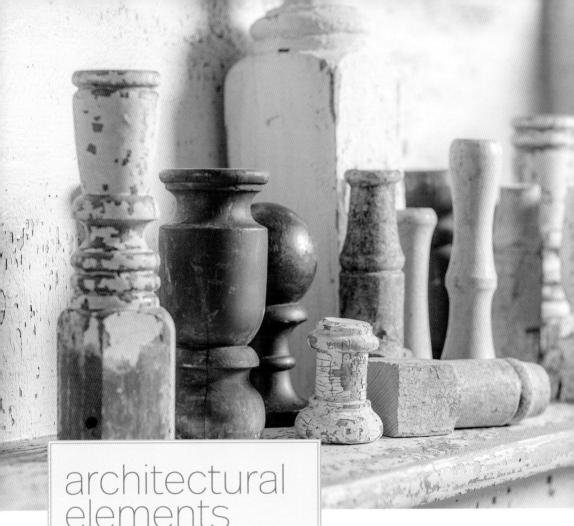

architectural elements

Salvaged architectural elements run the gamut from trendy and spendy to fabulous frugal finds, depending on where you come across them. These types of finials, posts, and bannister pieces are always on my radar when I'm out junking. As you peruse the pages of this book, you'll see that I use these pieces again and again as risers to lift other objects or for shape, color, and texture in a vignette. Tipped over or upright, they're a decorating must-have.

> 66
> Collecting a variety of colors and finishes allows me to incorporate these elements into myriad displays depending on the mood I want to set.
> 99

alarm clocks

If watches can be collector's items for fashion-minded folks, shouldn't alarm clocks be collectible for the home-fashion minded? In addition to hearkening back to my grandmother's bedside table, what attracts my attention to little timepieces are the variety of numbering styles, the many ways the faces are trimmed with metal, and the clever pedestals and stands.

candy molds

These can be tough to find (because they're usually smaller than I expect), but when you keep your eye out for candy molds you may be surprised by the plethora of sizes and shapes available. Choose to collect one type, such as rabbits, or maybe enjoy the trappings of a season such as Easter and collect bunny, chick, and egg molds. Rarely, you'll find two-piece molds with hinges or clips that join the pieces.

game pins

Skittle pins and mini bowling pins were sometimes parts of children's play sets, pub games, or carnival games of chance. You may even find juggling pins (which aren't really meant for standing upright like their skittle or bowling pin counterparts) mixed in with these collectibles. The charm of the smaller pins, the curvy cuteness, and the patina of well-loved pieces of the past draw me in.

wooden bowls

Repetition is something most of us yearn for in our everyday lives: the comfort of familiar voices, seasons, and patterns. The same holds true with home decor. There is something comforting about the repetition of shapes.

Stacks of items from large to small have been a designer go-to for years. If wooden bowls speak to your heart, start a collection by searching for stackable sizes, then tuck them into your decor as often as you can.

> "
> I'm a maker. And as such,
> I appreciate handmade items
> that are one-of-a-kind.
> The worn imperfections are
> appealing to me.
> "

pie funnels

British pie funnels are similar
to pie birds, used to help steam
escape from filled pie crusts. What
attracts me to them is their small
size and the glazing, crazing, and
intricate markings. Some look like
little vases. Try turning them over
and filling them with flowers for
a petite display. Here, displaying
them atop French custard cups
helps vary their heights.

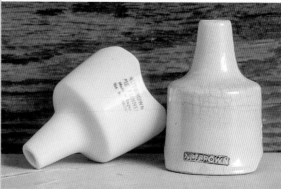

clock faces

Face it, what's not to love about clock faces? They're little round discs of artistry with numerals, intricate reliefs, and simple surfaces. Clock faces really shine when combined with mostly square shapes to add a pop of round contrast. Will they continue to be a hot commodity for collectors? Time will tell.

frames

There's a luscious texture and patina to old frames. I've been known to buy a picture just for the frame that surrounds it. Don't be afraid to discard the contents and keep only the frame! Most often, I leave the gnarled old wire on the back. I love how the wiry twists and curved lines play off the straight edges of the frames. (Finding frames with curved edges is a win as well!) It's all in the details. I'm always on the hunt for distinctive sizes and rich tactile features.

buttons

I inherited my mom's and grandmother's button collections in a gallon jar. I split them into smaller vessels—candy dishes and clear jars—so the buttons become the texture statement. There are so many ways to use buttons to soften an area. I like to incorporate them when I'm making a vignette or add a few to a handwork project.

Almost everyone can relate to a button collection as most people had a grandmother who saved buttons.

creamers

There's so much to love about creamers—the size, the multiple uses (cream, maple syrup, chocolate sauce), and the shapes. Ironstone without handles and just a hint of a spout is a favorite of mine for its simplicity, but a sassy little handle and wider spout catch my attention too. Tall and skinny, short and stout, simply striped, or monogrammed—I'm in for them all!

bottlebrush trees

If your style is more minimalist, you can't go wrong with
bottlebrush trees. These conical cuties are classic in shape
with clean lines. My collection is amped up with architectural
bases (you can find them with simpler circle disc stands, too).
Sticking to neutral tones for the trees adds a cool, relaxing vibe
that extends their use all winter.

candy boxes

When the packaging and messaging is as delightful as what used to be inside these sweet boxes, they truly are irresistible! Heart-shaped boxes win my heart every time, and when I find one with its original big bow, my heart skips a beat. Square and rectangular boxes make great risers in a display if they can't be shown face-out. Use these calorie-free cuties in your decor to add a fond memory of days gone by.

paintbrushes

The value of multiples of simple objects is easier to understand when you think about collections in terms of items such as paintbrushes. I prefer them dappled with paint, well worn, and a bit ruffled up. If you have 10 or 20 small brushes, picture a small loving cup filled with an artist's array. Large brushes showcase variations in bristles and shapes as if they're small sculptures.

57 BUTTERMILK ACRES

blue glass

Canning jars, sea floats, pharmaceutical jars, and old soda bottles—no matter the shape, blue glass catches the light on a sunny day like no other. Whether I'm after a resort-like beachy look, or a summery take-me-out-to-the-ball-game feeling, blue glass vessels and objects are the perfect hue to take your look from ordinary to extraordinary.

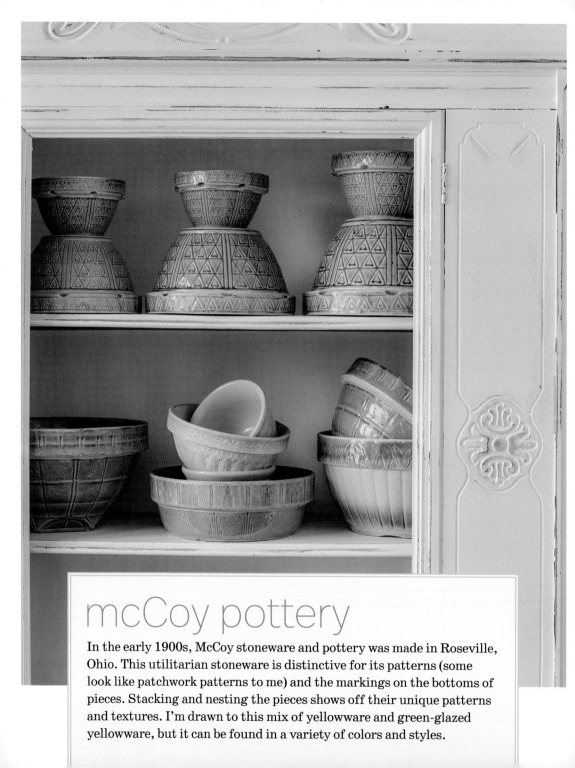

mcCoy pottery

In the early 1900s, McCoy stoneware and pottery was made in Roseville, Ohio. This utilitarian stoneware is distinctive for its patterns (some look like patchwork patterns to me) and the markings on the bottoms of pieces. Stacking and nesting the pieces shows off their unique patterns and textures. I'm drawn to this mix of yellowware and green-glazed yellowware, but it can be found in a variety of colors and styles.

shiny brites

These glass ornaments were wildly popular in the 1940s and 1950s. Named for the coating that made them stay shiny longer than other ornaments, Shiny Brites were the star attractions on many holiday trees. It's a great day when I find sets in their original boxes. I fill containers with ornaments and prop up full boxes among vignettes of holiday goodies. Patterned or solid colors, I love them all!

> *I consider cream vases a staple item to build into your collections. The neutral palette works with every season and adds elegance to an overall look.*

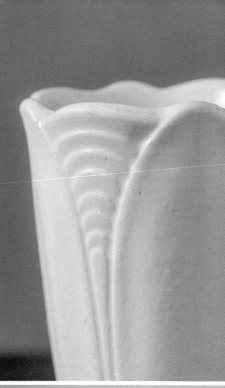

cream vases

I'm hard-pressed to pass by a cream-colored vase because I incorporate them into my decor in all seasons. How and what they're filled with can change the mood from rustic to refined. The artisanal craftsmanship displayed in the curves, details, and impressions takes my breath away. And the more pieces you collect, the more you can appreciate the simple elegance of a little cream vase. It's the little black dress of collector's items!

vintage
suitcases

If one suitcase is good, two are better, and five are downright delightful. What to hunt for? I'm smitten with ones that have stripes or houndstooth patterns. An interesting handle is always intriguing, as are original ID or travel tags. But the ones where the owner wrote the family name and address on the exterior really speak to me.

Bonus: you can use your suitcases to store out-of-season decor until you're ready to use it. Shhh, I won't tell.

COLLECTIONS

flower frogs

Intricate designs and interesting colors are what catch my eye when it comes to collecting flower frogs. I relish the variety of shapes and sizes and appreciate the mix of metals and clay options as well. Having a range of sizes and dimensions allows me to use several in a vignette, and the spiked ones are perfect holders for little ephemera such as old-time playing cards, flash cards, and vintage black-and-white photos. Or try tucking in a feather or single leaf.

66
Stack them, tip them, twist and turn them. There are no rules about using flower frogs as they were intended. Show off their curves and points!
99

clipboards

Call them what you will—a clipboard, receipt keeper, billing docket, thing that holds paper things—they're practically perfect in every way. I love to tuck mine into vignettes on tabletops, hang them on the wall, and tilt them atop easels. They can hold bits of ephemera, love notes, business cards, little paintings, and other favorite finds. They're fun and functional!

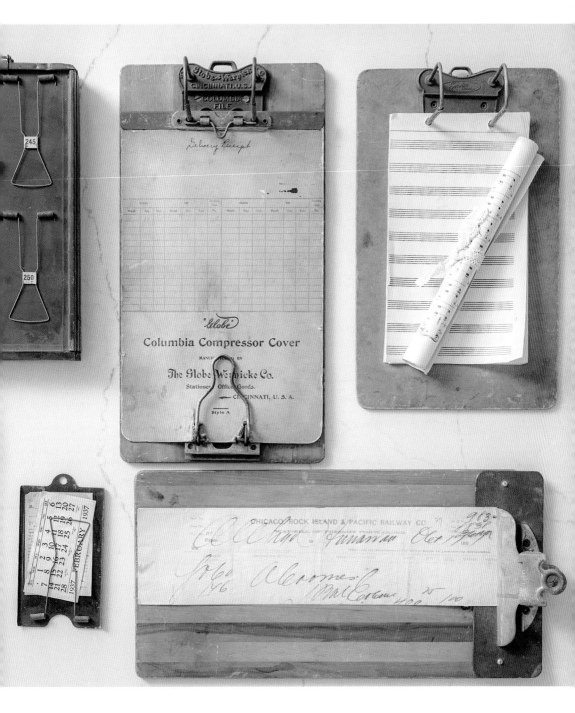

scales

Weight, weight, don't touch that dial! Nothing moves the needle like finding a scale that still has a working spring. Drugstore scales, candy scales, grocery scales, and kitchen scales all exude a solid, timeworn appeal with their artful hands and variety of mechanisms. Perch a favorite find atop a scale as a pedestal of sorts, to elevate its importance.

sock stretchers

Wooden sock stretchers come in all shapes and sizes because they were in fact used in many households (as their name suggests) to prevent all sizes of stockings from shrinking after washing. Stretchers kept them the right size and shape, and the holes helped air flow through for faster drying. The mix of lengths and widths adds a bit of whimsy to a collection's display.

baskets

You can fill them, stack them, hang them, tip them, and nest them. The colors and styles range from modern to traditional, rustic to refined. Choose the ones that speak to your heart for their shape, their maker, their story. Maybe it's the artfully crafted widths used in the weave that draws you in. When you have four or more, you have a collection.

egg baskets

The intricacies and details of French egg baskets are stunning. Made from wire, some have handles that open and close to secure the eggs, others stand alone. And many have decorative scallops. I also collect vintage eggs in wood, glass, and speckled varieties. The milk glass eggs were put into nests to encourage chickens to lay their eggs.

platters

When you're a collector, finding ways to
display your wares can be a challenge. That's
the beauty of platters. They can sit anywhere
at any time! Stack them on a side table,
center them on an island, or place them atop
a bookshelf. The concentric rings look great
if you stack them on a low surface you can see
from above. Use the top platter as a display
spot for a favorite trinket, or to catch your
keys just inside the entry.

cabinet drawers

You had me at multiple drawers. The only thing better than finding a little vintage, slightly worn cabinet with multiple drawers is finding one with drawers in different sizes. These pieces check all the boxes for me. From full-sized furniture to tiny doll-sized cabinet drawers, I use them in lots of ways: drawers shut, drawers open, even drawers upside-down to make shelves!

open cubbies

Cubbies are a free-for-all opportunity to showcase collections. Different styles appeal to different people, so think about what you love and what you want to showcase. Do you need symmetry in the openings? Do you prefer a mix of horizontal and vertical spaces? My preference is for cubbies that aren't much deeper than 4", otherwise treasures get lost in the shadows. But then a nesting box catches my eye and all bets are off!

chippy paint

Maybe chippy painted objects don't really count as a collection . . . or maybe they do. Beauty is definitely in the eye of the beholder, but in my world, the chippier the better. Not only do those cracks and chips share a little behind-the-scenes story with my vintage-loving heart, but they also mean I don't have to worry about using them. If they get chipped or scratched up a bit, who will know? It's a win-win!

> *Looking at chippy paint is like looking at the history of a piece—where its been, how many colors its worn. The aged patina adds rich texture.*

resources

Some of my favorite shops, Instagram accounts, and special events are listed below, but this really is the tip of the iceberg. When I travel, I do a quick search on my phone for antique shops, architectural salvage, and eclectic home-decor boutiques along my route and at the destination. Building in a little extra time in my schedule to check out the spots I find has led me to some wonderful, one-of-a-kind discoveries.

FAVORITE SHOPS

» Haupt Antiek
Apple Valley, Minnesota

» Shop 501 & Company
Chaska, Minnesota

» Urban Cottage
Minneapolis, Minnesota

» The Findery
Waco, Texas

» Good Ju Ju
Kansas City, Missouri

» Loot Vintage & Supply
Waupaca, Wisconsin

» Miss Lucille's Marketplace
Clarksville, Tennessee

» The Old Lucketts Store
Leesburg, Virginia

SPECIAL EVENTS

» Junk Bonanza
Shakopee, Minnesota

» The Farm Chicks Vintage &
Handmade Fair
Spokane, Washington

» Junk Jubilee
Des Moines, Iowa

» Main Street Market—Urban Farmgirl
Belvidere, Illinois

» Marburger Farm Antique Show
Round Top, Texas

» Vintage Pickin
Fort Payne, Alabama

MUST-SEE INSTAGRAM ACCOUNTS

» @CottageHome_cathscadden

» @theCottonShed

» @EastEndSalvage

» @TheFeatheredNest1

» @HavenberryVintage

» @HoggBarnAntiques

» @HollingsworthandCo

» @JBSMercantile

» @KilgoresVintageDesign

» @SouthPorch

» @ten_mile_supply

» @VintageGreenAntiques

dedication

Everything I've accomplished is a result of the love my family shares with me.

My mother, Linda, and my grandmas, Lily and Avis, were my earliest influencers. Much of what I collect is reminiscent of growing up surrounded by and engaged in their creativity.

My husband, George, is my number one man and fan all rolled into one. His support of my wild ideas never wavers. He's always up for a road trip or an adventure with me. He hangs the sun and the moon in my eyes.

Our daughters, Hannah and Grace, have grown up watching my passion for collecting and creating memorable places throughout our home. As young adults now, it delights me to have them join me on a junking trip or pull me aside to tell me to put their name on an item they hope to inherit. They are my stars and I'm proud to be their mom.